```
HV          Harrity, Anne Swany
5824
.C45        Kids, drugs &
H37         alcohol
1987
649.4 H323
```

SSCC - GILL'

Memphis and Shelby County Public Library and Information Center

For the Residents
of
Memphis and Shelby County

KIDS, DRUGS, & ALCOHOL

A Parent's Guide to Prevention & Intervention

**Anne Swany Harrity
Ann Brey Christensen**

BETTERWAY PUBLICATIONS, INC.
White Hall, Virginia

Published by Betterway Publications, Inc.
Box 74
White Hall, VA 22987

Cover design by Deborah B. Chapell
Cover photograph by Charles H. Lane
Typography by East Coast Typography, Inc.

Copyright © 1987 by Anne Harrity and Ann Christensen

All rights reserved. No part of this book may be reproduced by any means, except by a reviewer who wishes to quote brief excerpts in connection with a review in a magazine or newspaper.

Library of Congress Cataloging-in-Publication Data

Harrity, Anne Swaney, 1938-
   Kids, drugs, and alcohol.

   Includes bibliographies and index.
   1. Children — United States — Drug Use.   2. Children — United States — Alcohol Use.   3. Drug abuse — United States — Prevention. I. Christensen, Ann, 1941-   II. Title.   1. Alcohol Drinking — in adolescence — popular works.   2. Drugs — popular works.   3. Substance Abuse — in adolescence — popular works.   WM 270 H323k]
HV5824.C45H37   1987   649'.4   87-7994
ISBN 0-932620-74-4 (pbk.)

Printed in the United States of America
0987654321

Our personal commitment to the fight against teenage drug and alcohol abuse was initially motivated by Colorado newspaper headlines:

CAR HITS RIVER; 5 PAONIA TEENS DIE

GREELEY TEEN KILLED AFTER 'KEG PARTY'

TEEN-AGER KILLED IN BEER PARTY FIGHT

SCHOOL PILL-POPPING BINGE
SENDS KIDS TO HOSPITAL

POLICE PIN TEEN'S DEATH TO DRINKING

We therefore dedicate this book to America's "parents movement," which is devoted to keeping headlines like these out of individual communities across the country.

Acknowledgements

We extend our deepest appreciation to the following corporations and individuals whose supportive assistance and generosity in sharing resources, information and ideas has made this guidelines booklet a hard-copy reality.

CORPORATE ACKNOWLEDGEMENTS

Corporate Graphics
IBM Corporation
Kemper Group
Public Service Company of Colorado

INDIVIDUAL ACKNOWLEDGEMENTS

Special thanks to Mr. Tom Brewster, MSW, Associate Director, and Thomas J. Crowley, M.D., Executive Director, of Addiction Research and Treatment Services, University of Colorado Health Sciences Center.

Also our thanks to Arapahoe County District Attorney Mr. H. Michael Steinberg; Mr. Donald O. Cramer; Mr. Michael Sabbeth; Mr. Charles Richardson; Aurora Municipal Court Judge Loretta Huffine; members of the Aurora Police Department, especially Lieutenant Tom Cornelius, Division Chief Jerry Fricke (Ret.), Agent Paul Grey, Lieutenant Tom Maron, Officer Scott Weaver, Agent Ted Wiggin; Ms. Donna Shear, Publisher of the Aurora Sentinel; Big Brothers, Inc. and Mr. Bert Singleton; Dr. Ken Ash and Mr. Armon Johannsen of CAP Task Force, Fort Collins, CO.

Members of the Cherry Creek School District were extremely supportive of our efforts. We would particularly like to acknowledge Dr. Donald K. Goe; Ms. Helen Bess; Dr. Bill Porter; Mr. Joseph Adamo; Ms. Tamara Bauer; Mr. Ed Ellis; Dr. Fred Henderson; Ms. Diana Stevens; Ms. Nancy Day; Ms. Leslie Hatfield. We appreciate also the input of Overland High School students: Mr. Tim Carter, Ms. Heather Dowd, Mr. Jim Luthi, Ms. Ginger Margolin, Mr. Bryan Webb, Ms. Kirstin Weidemueller. Overland Task Force for Alcohol/Drug Free Youth, especially Ms. Margie Barnes, Ms. Linda Burniston, Mr. Joe Dowd, Mr. Pete Harrity, Mr. Rick Kissinger, Ms. Jean Thayer, Ms. Vicki Webb. Cherry Creek Task Force on Youth and Drugs, including Ms. Brownie Harvey, Ms. Brenda Holben, Ms. Sherry Sargent.

Colorado Division of Highway Safety's Mr. Phillip J. Weiser; Ms. Dee Melander, Director, and Mr. Bill Melander of Colorado SADD; Mr. Michael Collum, Director of Colorado Teen Institute; Ms. Joan P. Herst of The Denver Post; Department of Revenue Investigators Jim Berry and Dan Sinawski; Charles E. Llewellyn, Jr., M.D., Head of Duke University's Division of Social and Community Psychiatry; Mr. Jim Porter, Executive Director of Mile High Council on Alcoholism; Ms. Lynda Brian of Mountain Area Families in Action (MAFIA); Mr. George Anderson, R.Ph.; Mr. Gary Buss, R.Ph.; Dr. David E. Dangerfield, DSW; Mr. Michael H. Shaffer, MSW; 7-Eleven Stores' Ms. Mary Boyd, Store Manager, and Ms. Marti Greeson, Security Division; Smoky Hill High School Parent Information Network, Ms. Dee Gordon; University of Denver Professor Nicholas Braucht; Mr. Dan Morgan of The Washington Post; Western Insurance Information Service, Area Director Ms. Cheryl Malvestuto; Young Life, Area Director Mr. John Hartle.

Ms. Carol Boigon, Aurora Sentinel; Ms. Jane Hulse, Rocky Mountain News; Ms. June Perryman, Parents Who Care, Inc.; Ms. Jan Strege; Ms. Becky Clamp; Ms. Joanne Stribling; Ms. Anne Feely and Ms. Jann Glatz, Substance Abuse Counselors.

Parents! Do You Know?

Current opinion polls indicate that drug abuse has surpassed economic woes and the threat of war as the nation's number 1 concern. Dr. Kenneth Shonberg, Director of Adolescent Medicine, Montefiore Hospital, Bronx, New York, states that abuse of liquor and marijuana is the leading cause of death for adolescents in the United States. This includes alcohol or marijuana related fatalities.

———————— ABOUT ALCOHOL ————————

- One in every four American teenagers will become a problem drinker in high school.
- Nearly 30% of 4th graders experience pressure to try alcohol.
- 33.4% of the nation's 6th graders have tried beer or wine and 9.5% have tried hard liquor. Alcohol use among 6th graders more than doubled from 1983-87.
- The single leading cause of death among 15-24 year olds is drinking and driving.
- 43% of 7th graders have experimented with beer and wine; 23% with hard liquor.
- Many teenagers today, including a high percentage of teenage athletes, say they drink primarily to get high, rather than to relax or to help them socialize.
- The arrest rate for drunkenness among children under 18 has tripled in the past ten years.
- Teenage drinkers are several times more likely to become problem drinkers or use other mind-altering drugs than non-drinkers. Ten thousand teenagers die each year in alcohol-related accidents of some type.

ABOUT OTHER GATEWAY DRUGS

- 25% of 4th graders say they feel pressured to try drugs.
- 11% of 6th graders start using drugs while in 6th grade.
- About two out of three American young people have tried an illicit drug before they finish high school.
- The average age a child starts marijuana use is 13.
- Among 12th graders, 54% say they have tried marijuana.
- One in ten seniors and one in 13 juniors use cocaine occasionally to daily.
- The number of "crack" users is increasing at a rate of 2,000 per day (many of them teenagers).
- Most middle school kids know who the drug dealers are in the community.
- Middle school kids who use drugs say they were turned on to them not only by dealers, but also by older teenage friends, older siblings and their friends, baby sitters and adult relatives.
- In an average classroom, one child in four is from a substance abusing household.

Contents

Introduction 11

1. Facts About Adolescents 13

    Characteristics of the Typical Adolescent, 13
    Adolescent Susceptibility — Why?, 17

2. Facts About Drugs and Their Effects 19

    Points to Ponder, 19
    Facts about Alcohol, 23
    Facts about Nicotine
        (All-Tobacco and Clove Cigarettes, Snuff), 27
    Facts about Marijuana, 29
    Facts about Cocaine and Crack, 31
    Facts about Designer Drugs, 37
    Adverse Reactions from Combining
        Alcohol with Other Drugs, 39

3. The Teen Social Scene 41

    "Hangin' Out" and Other Social "Happenings", 41
    "Keg Parties" and Other Beer Busts, 48
    The Kegger Scenario, 49
    Teenage Drinking and Driving, 58

4. Practical Prevention 67

    The Case Against Teenage Drinking, 67
    Strategies of Prevention, 70
    Notes For Single Parents (and Stepparents), 87
    Suggested Parenting Guidelines, 89
    Alternate Activities, 92
    Letting Go, 92
    Creating a Personal Challenge, 97

5. Intervention 99

Where Does Intervention Begin?, 99
When and How Does Use Become Abuse —
  Then What?, 101
"Red Flags" of Adolescent Drug Involvement, 104
Adolescent Problem Drinkers Compared
  to Other Adolescents, 106
Experimentation — Suggested Actions, 107
Dealing with Recreational Users, 112
A Look at the More Advanced User, 115

6. Counseling, Treatment and Aftercare 119

Denial, 119
The Decision to Get Help — A Difficult One!, 120
When the Situation Is Out of Control, 122
Types of Available Treatment, 125
The Problem of Aftercare. 130

7. For Kids Only 135

A Personal Checklist, 135
When a Friend Has a Problem with Drugs, 136
When a Friend's Parent Has
  a Problem with Drugs, 137
Handling Peer Pressure and Drugs, 138
Suggested Precautions from Law
  Enforcement Agencies, 139

Appendices 143

A. Controlled Substances: Uses & Effects, 144
B. Awareness Test For Parents, 146
C. Specific Signs and
   Symptoms of Adolescent Drug Use, 148
D. Stages in Adolescent Chemical Use, 150
E. How to Give a Successful Teenage Party, 151
F. What You Can Expect if
   Your Child is Arrested, 153
G. Potential Legal Liabilities of
   the "Kegger Scenario", 154
H. An Open Letter to Parents and
   Teenage Drivers, 158
I. Sample Contingency Contract, 161
J. Sample Substance Abuse Policy and Procedure, 162
K. Additional Resources and Reading, 171

Index 175

About the Authors 180

Introduction

Many of us who were the teenagers of the fifties and sixties find ourselves in the eighties as parents of teenagers. Often we hear other adults, and perhaps even ourselves, saying derisively, "Today's generation of teenagers is *different* — not like we were as teenagers!" What do we find so different about the teenagers of the eighties? They are trying to identify self and establish autonomy. Their adolescent self-esteem is fragile. They want to "hang out" together. They want to be liked by their peers. They want to be "cool." They want to prove that they are *not* children. Yet, they still want to love and be loved.

Is this not a very apt description of ourselves when we were teenagers twenty (plus or minus) years ago? When we were kids, we took risks. We pushed ourselves and our luck. We survived our sophomoric adventures — often by the skin of our teeth — to become parents ourselves. The main difference between us as teenagers and our own teenagers seems to be that, today, satisfying these perfectly normal needs involves making a choice about using alcohol and other drugs. Teenagers of the eighties, unlike their parents, have had easy access to alcohol and other drugs from a very early age. Thus, our *teenagers* aren't so very different. It is *society* that is different!

Many of our children are experimenting with drugs that were relatively unknown a generation ago. The long-term effects of some are still unknown. There is enormous peer pressure confronting them on this issue. Overdose, wasted, wired, buzzed, spaced-out, blasted, stoned — all comprise a new litany of terms relevant to our children's generation. And we parents, many of us not having experienced an adolescent drug scene, often don't know when our children have a problem — much less what to do about it.

This guide proposes to help fill the gap in preventive education. It does not presume to be a do-it-yourself drug/alcohol manual. Rather, it is designed to acquaint parents with the scope of the issue, target specific social problems (such as keg parties), provide basic information about some of the drugs most commonly used and abused by teenagers and offer practical suggestions for prevention, early detection and intervention.

If, after reading this book, you feel that your teenager might have a serious problem, **GET HELP!** Your family doctor or pediatrician is an excellent place to start. Some potential sources of help are listed in the appendix. You can find other sources listed in the Yellow Pages of the phone book under "Alcoholism" and "Drug Addiction."

EVEN IF YOUR CHILD IS *NOT* THE ONE IN EVERY TEN TEENAGERS TODAY WHO IS ADDICTED to a chemical substance, he or she is still adversely affected by the fallout from this teenage epidemic. Whether your teenager is a non-user, an experimenter, or a regular user, he or she desperately needs your understanding, your support, your guidance and your constant reinforcement.

REMEMBER! A child's best weapon against alcohol and drugs is an informed parent! Get involved before your kids do!

1. Facts About Adolescents

CHARACTERISTICS OF THE TYPICAL ADOLESCENT*

Self-conscious

The central theme of adolescence is the finding of oneself.

The adolescent must become acquainted with a whole new body and somehow fit this new body into an image of himself. It is this search for familiarity with his own physical features that accounts for the extreme number of hours spent before the mirror in the bathroom.

The intensified self-awareness is manifested by a high degree of self-consciousness. At this age level, individual differences between himself and his peer group now become more clear-cut than they were at an earlier age. His own uniqueness, still only half understood, is not completely welcomed.

The adolescent's self-consciousness comes from having to find an identity within himself rather than as a member of a family or of a peer group. It can be said, therefore, that while the younger adolescent is concerned with who and what he is, the older adolescent is more concerned with what to do about it.

In Conflict with His Family

If the adolescent is to secure separateness from his family, a separate definition of himself, he must break family ties. By breaking family ties, we mean he has to separate himself from family authority, affection, support, intimacy, and possessiveness, not to mention family habits and traditions. The parents

---

*From *Aggressive Adolescents* by David E. Dangerfield, DSW, and Michael H. Shaffer, MSW, Professional Training Associates. Excerpt with permission of the authors.

[13]

and the adolescent are at war with each other, but the adolescent is also at war with himself due to his terrific ambivalence about the desirability of growing up.

If parents interfere in the adolescent's life, they are snoopy and domineering; if they do not interfere, they are unfeeling and "just don't care or understand."

Parents, while damned if they do and damned if they don't, still need to provide limits as something tangible for the adolescent to fight as well as to provide the adolescent a feeling of stability and security.

Fiercely Attached to His Peer Group

The adolescent peer group differs from the childhood peer group, as the adolescent group no longer views itself as part of childhood society, but instead as a "new kind of adult society." Adolescents do not view themselves as becoming adult like their parents, but instead feel a uniqueness to their maturity which differentiates them from the adults in their world.

The beginning of adolescence is the high point in the rejection of adults. All of us adults are included, except, perhaps, that one unusual parent, coach, or adult leader whom the kids choose to view differently. As the adolescent moves through adolescence, he moves from the same sex peer group to an opposite sex allegiance and from the neighborhood group to a wider geographic group which dramatically increases in size with the security of a driver's license, which increases mobility.

Adolescents are all "running for office," in the sense that they need recognition from their peers to tell them where they stand. High school populations break into cliques, which are based on personality types and abilities, e.g., jocks, intellectuals, etc.

Adolescents are so unsure of themselves that they go to great lengths to shun the unpopular students around them, as if they may be infectious, and instead cultivate relationships with the popular, hoping the popularity will "rub off" on them.

Seeking Conformity and Popularity

For the adolescent, rigid conformity is the rule. The phenomenon could be called the Conformity Neurosis: in its most extreme form we see adolescents risk even death to maintain a place within the peer group.

The search for a personality is often less of a search for an inter-security than it is a search for gimmicks or tricks that might make people like them. Adolescents cannot be satisfied with what they *are*. They need someone on the outside to tell them they are all right, and the louder the approval, the more the reinforcement, the better. The occasional adolescent who is not concerned with popularity finds his peers flocking around him like a tower of strength, hungry for that sense of self-assurance.

Of interest is the fact that parents are often completely ignorant of the standards by which adolescents choose "who to be in with." Parents, try as they might, continue to be bewildered by their adolescent's choice of friends and the fierce loyalty he gives to them.

Preoccupied with Bodily Changes

Adolescence is a time of physical awkwardness, of shaving peach fuzz, and measuring height almost daily. It is a time made up of weight-lifting, buying training bras, changing voices, hairstyles, and becoming extremely aware of one's looks, one's complexion, and one's physical attractiveness.

The adolescent's notions about themselves are deeply embedded in the impressions they have of their own bodies. While this phenomenon is true for all of us, it is much more accentuated in adolescence than in adulthood. Almost universally, adolescents will judge themselves very harshly with regard to their physical attractiveness, while adults have normally settled into an appreciation (or at least acceptance) of their bodies and their overall appearances. The adolescent's body is his facade to the world, so it is enormously important. Typically, adolescents are not objective appraisers of themselves and focus only on those ways in which they do not meet any "ideal image."

Trying to Create a Personality

The adolescent's search is not so much trying to find something that is there as much as it is trying to create something that isn't there — a personality. The adolescent tries different dress styles, hand-shakes, voices, handwriting, greetings, and manners; he emulates others until he finds a set of behaviors that seem to fit. The adolescent experiments to discover what various styles feel like to him and what responses they elicit from others. Every new personality is to be assumed totally and cannot be questioned.

The personality used last week is discarded as if it never was. The adolescent, however, cannot feel the part he plays unless he gets a reaction from those of us around him. The more people take him for granted, the less he is able to take himself for granted. The adult task, then, is to give "feedback" by reacting honestly to the changing personality.

By late adolescence, hopefully, the young person is coming together into the "real me", which changes less violently with time.

Trying to Keep the Sexual Lid On

For all adolescents, there is the universal feeling of embarrassment, the fear that one might let slip at the wrong moment the thoughts that are preoccupying him.

It is a time to sort out the difficult and conflicting cultural messages: "Sex is dirty; save it for someone you love," or its counterpart, "Sex is beautiful; just don't tell my children about it."

The adolescent boy's sexual focus is highly specific, centering in the genital area. With girls, the focus is more diffuse. For boys, the sexual craving is separate from love. For girls, the two of them work more closely together.

The sexual part of our being is perhaps the most basic aspect there is, requiring the adolescent to give it attention and time. It is essential to overall identity formation.

Idealistic

The adolescent's search for philosophical roots stems from the common theme of searching for oneself and for one's place in the world.

Often, the adolescent's idealism is hidden from his peers as well as from his family, especially his parents. It is because his parents do not recognize this part of him that the adolescent criticizes them by saying, "You just don't understand me."

Idealism is manifested in the adolescent's quest for sincerity and honesty between people. It is the same idealism that prompts long walks, the writing of poetry, or the solitary hours with the earphones on. It is the same idealism which prompts his genuine sympathy for humanity at large.

The adolescent may be deeply attuned to the down-trodden or the oppressed and may seem to search for "causes" to which he reacts with great emotion. On the same basis, many adolescents are highly attracted to the idealism of religion, some to pageantry, some to militancy, and some to the simplicity of the blacks and whites and right and wrongs. The adolescent's concern with religion is part and parcel of his concern with the nature of the world into which he is moving so that the nature and the existence of God and the need for faith are among the topics endlessly debated among adolescents in bull sessions.

Most young people by late adolescence have pretty much come to terms with "things as they are," and can then put more energy into the tasks of "living and providing," as ultimately required in adulthood.

—— ADOLESCENT SUSCEPTIBILITY —— WHY?

Why not? If the symptoms of adolescence were to appear in a person of any other age, it would be diagnosed as a disease. Let's examine the symptoms from an adult perspective — as if they were suffered by a close adult friend.

- ✔ We see a person with very fragile self-esteem undergoing a painful identity crisis.

- ✔ He (or she) is subject to extreme and uncontrollable mood swings due, in part, to a temporary hormonal imbalance.

- ✔ At a time when he is almost paranoid about his appearance, he is vulnerable to dramatic and sudden physical changes, many of which are not at all attractive — acne, gawkiness, incoordination, etc.

Even though the adolescent desperately needs family support to cope with his situation, he may appear compelled to sever the umbilical cord which, he feels, constrictively binds him to his parents. Yet, once the cord is cut or sufficiently weakened, he may be willing to toss away his hard-fought independence in a struggle to gain security and acceptance within the womb of a peer family. Unhappily, he may discover that the peer family demands even stricter conformity.

If he is fortunate, he will hook-up with a compatible peer group that will positively complement his inadequacies and assist him in the maturation process. On the other hand, the members of his new peer group may be obviously immature, contrary to his basic principles, dictatorial and even abusive. But like the battered spouse, he may choose to live with it and continue to actively seek favor because he sees no viable alternative at the moment.

At the same time the adolescent is struggling with these personal relationships, he must face the increasing reality of day to day living. The responsibilities of secondary school are not child's play. He discovers new "necessities" in his life. Money, transportation, alternative actions begin to pose problems. Each day brings another mundane problem to the surface.

All of these perplexities coupled with the private conflicts regarding emerging sexuality, idealistic disillusionment, and getting in touch with feelings would result in unbearable stress for most adults. How much more so for the less sophisticated and less mature adolescent? An adult, in the midst of any one of these traumatic crises, might be sorely tempted to relax, or even temporarily escape, from the relentless stress of the situation with a prescription for Valium or a few martinis — both common and socially acceptable adult methods of coping with stress.

Teenagers today also have easy access to alcohol and other drugs, and many of them feel ill-equipped at a particular moment to otherwise cope with stress, anger, fear, insecurity, peer pressure, etc. From age 15 on, alcohol and marijuana use is taken as the social norm in most communities. Teenagers who don't participate become increasingly a minority as they move into the upper classes. And so the question arises, "Why not?"

2. Facts About Drugs and Their Effects

---------- POINTS TO PONDER ----------

The teen drug and alcohol situation in your community is probably accurately reflected in the national statistics, which tell us that the majority of American teenagers start alcohol use between the ages of 11 and 14. The average age that a child starts marijuana use is 13. Recently, spurred by lower prices, cocaine use has started moving into the nation's high schools. Facts like these raise a broad spectrum of questions, including some concerning the correlation between drug use and various other teenage issues.

What Are The Teenage Drugs?

A drug is any chemical substance that brings about physical, emotional, or mental changes in people. Alcohol, tobacco, aspirin and even caffeine (in coffee, tea, cocoa, and cola drinks) are drugs. Other less widely used drugs include THC (in marijuana and hashish), amphetamines, barbituates, tranquilizers, narcotics, cocaine, phencyclidine (PCP), volatile chemicals (glue and other inhalants), and LSD. A chart of controlled substances, their uses and effects appears in Appendix A.

According to a drug use survey conducted annually for the National Institute on Drug Abuse (NIDA) by the University of Michigan Institute for Social Research (The High School Senior Survey), there is a definite trend in teenage drug use. The 1985 survey involved more than 16,000 high school seniors from public and private schools. It showed alcohol to be the most popular drug, followed in order by tobacco, marijuana/hashish, stimulants and cocaine.

Robert L. DuPont, M.D., President of the Center for Behavioral Medicine and former director of NIDA, says, "Three drugs have become the gateways into the drug-dependence syndrome in

America — alcohol is the gateway into use of chemically induced intoxication, marijuana is the gateway into illicit drug use, and cocaine is the gateway into intensified illicit drug use. These drugs act as gateways because they are widely — and wrongly — seen as harmless and easily controlled by the user." This observation on three of the drugs most popular with America's teenagers was made in Dr. DuPont's article entitled "Marijuana, Alcohol and Adolescence: A Malignant Synergism," which appeared in the October 25, 1985 *Journal of the American Medical Association*.

Who Is At Risk?

In introducing the 1987 CHEMICAL PEOPLE II television documentary, "Generation at Risk," First Lady Nancy Reagan states that the terrifying specter of teenage alcohol and drug abuse with its related problems (e.g., teen pregnancy, suicide, dropping out of school, delinquent behavior, etc.) threatens the health and happiness of an *entire generation* — the nation's children. No family is immune. However, some children appear to be more at risk than others. The following, for example, are considered more likely to use alcohol and other drugs: male youths, teenagers who have a circle of friends who drink or use other drugs, adolescents who experience repeated failures, children from dysfunctional families.

Among adolescents who already use chemical substances there are other risks to consider. For example, teenagers are thought to become addicted to the drug alcohol more quickly than adults. Children of alcoholics run a biological risk for alcoholism four times greater than children of non-alcoholic parents. Examine these risk factors in relation to *your* children.

Why Would Your Child Use Alcohol And Other Drugs?

Youths, particularly in their early teen years, use drugs for a multitude of specific personal reasons. Whatever the reason, he or she considers the immediate rewards far more important than the long-term risks — addiction, death by overdose and drunk driving, for example. There are, though, several general reasons for drug use which can be identified.

- Availability. If it's always around, why not try it?
- Curiosity coupled with a desire to experiment with any current fad.
- Social influences of peers, relatives and media pressure.

- A desire to appear and/or feel "grown up" and independent.
- A desire for attention, which is erroneously equated with popularity.
- A need to be one's own person which may, consciously or subconsciously, be an attempt to rebel against authority.
- A means of expressing anger and/or seeking revenge against parents.
- A desire to enhance pleasure or seek the thrill/excitement of risk.
- An inability to cope with reality, accompanied by a need to block the stress caused by grades, peer relationships, parent problems, etc.
- A need to dull the pain caused by "bad" feelings (e.g., low self-esteem, loneliness, fear, anger, guilt, resentment, etc.)

Alcohol, Other Drugs And Teenage Sex

According to national statistics released in conjunction with CHEMICAL PEOPLE II four out of every ten girls will become pregnant while still in their teens. The age of first intercourse is 16.2 years, dropping to 15.5 years in urban/minority populations. One-fourth of all sexually transmitted disease victims are still in high school.

A Colorado survey on teenage sexual activity taken bi-annually in the Jefferson County School District consistently shows results within a few percentage points of national norms. Students who have had sexual intercourse say that 83% of the time they were under the influence of alcohol or marijuana. Those students who admit to having had intercourse include 9% of 6th graders compared with 22% of 8th graders. By 12th grade the number increases to 46% of the girls and 40% of the boys. Seventy-six percent of these students report that the sexual activity occurred in one of their homes — more in the boys than in the girls.

Alcohol, Other Drugs And Teenage Suicide

In the United States, the suicide rate of young people (15-24) has tripled over the past 30 years. An American teenager commits suicide nearly every 90 minutes. For every suicide reported, there are 50 to 100 attempts. Many of these, although certainly not all, might be considered casualties of "life in the fast lane." More than half of all adolescent suicides are drug related.

Why would a young person try to take his or her own life? Child specialists note that even though adolescents have always gone through physical and emotional upheavals, today's adolescents may be under even more pressure. This generation is faced with more choices, greater freedom and fewer limits than ever before. Normal teenage depression may be intensified by: family crisis, divorce, death of a parent or friend, peer pressure, parental pressure to achieve, a failed romance or friendship, a move to a new neighborhood or school, a learning disability, etc. Nationally, the majority of teenage suicide attempts are precipitated by a problem with parents; one-third involve members of the opposite sex.

Alcohol and other drugs are often used by teenagers as a *temporary* solution to their problems. Many drugs, including alcohol, are further depressants and may cause some of those same teens to seek death as a *final* solution because such temporary measures have failed. For still others, chemical substances may have clouded their minds to the point they don't fully comprehend that they won't be around for the "put-down" that their family and friends will suffer or the attention that their suicide will attract. Without the mind altering chemical substance which tends to curtail communication skills, among other things, perhaps they could have been helped to come to a realization of their own individual worth and their unlimited capacity to change, grow and solve problems.

How Effective Is "Drug Facts" Education In Our Schools?

Knowing facts about alcohol and other drugs does not deter teenagers from experimenting with drugs. Many teenagers feel what they were taught in elementary school about the harmful effects of drugs, particularly alcohol, was just a "scare tactic." They feel nothing is *going* to happen to them because nothing *has* happened. There is no immediate evidence of the threatened long-term negative effects. Thus, they feel that as individuals they are more powerful than the negative effects of the drugs.

If there is pressure to experiment, drug facts alone will not change a student's mind. One Colorado educator suggests that the key to effective drug education is to include information on effective ways to deal with the pressure to experiment. She suggests that students need assertiveness training to learn alternate ways of saying, "no." In addition, students should be taught coping strategies, stress management, communication, and other peer pressure reversal skills.

How Educated Are Parents About "Drug Facts"?

Many parents know *some* basic facts about drugs, but few are very knowledgeable about *current* drug facts and how they relate to the adolescent. It is only in recent years that adolescent use of alcohol and other drugs has reached epidemic proportions at younger and younger ages, and the effects on teenagers have been studied in depth.

Chemical substances such as cocaine, which were not a major part of the sixties drug scene, have surfaced and found favor with teenagers. The paraphernalia industry, unknown fifteen years ago, is booming. Drugs of the sixties, such as marijuana, have become much more available, more varied, more potent and therefore, more dangerous. After years of concentrated study, the researchers are only now getting hard evidence of the long-term negative effects of some of these drugs. Parents *should* know about them.

——————— FACTS ABOUT ALCOHOL ———————

Statistics

Alcohol is the chemical substance most used and abused by teenagers today. Even though state laws prohibit the purchase and/or consumption of all alcoholic beverages by those under a certain age (18-21), the teenagers in our country manage to obtain it easily by using false IDs, asking people of legal age to purchase it for them, or by other more imaginative means.

National statistics for 1985 indicate that 1 in 20 high school seniors drink alcohol daily. This is down from 1 in 16 three years ago. Two-thirds of the seniors surveyed had used alcohol at least once in the 30 days prior to the survey. Only 8% reported they had never used alcohol. In the 1987 public television documentary "Generation at Risk," Nancy Reagan stated that one out of every four American teenagers would become a problem drinker while in high school.

Teenage drinking varies from community to community and even from school to school, but it is reasonable to assume that if local statistics were available, they would indicate a *similar trend in your own community*. Call your state's Department of Health and inquire about the statistics relating to your specific area. However, remember that accurate comparisons of different studies are often difficult due to a lack of uniformity in various stages of data handling.

Alcohol — The Drug

Alcohol is indeed a drug — the most used and abused drug in America! It not only can cause social destruction, disease and accidents, but also addiction and irreversible damage to brain cells. Yet it is such an integral part of American life that many parents consider teenage alcohol experimentation both innocent and harmless. Their reaction to teenage drinking is "oh, thank goodness, they're not into 'drugs'."

Ethyl alcohol, the most active ingredient in wine, beer and distilled liquor, is a natural substance formed by the reaction of fermenting sugar with yeast spores. It is colorless, inflammable and intoxicating. In small doses it acts as a temporary stimulant and/or has a calming effect, but it is basically a central nervous system depressant. In fact, removing the water from ethyl alcohol produces ether, a general anesthetic used in surgery to put patients to sleep. An excessive drinking bout or combining alcohol with other depressants may result in respiratory arrest and heart failure. These adverse reactions are described at the end of this section.

ALCOHOL CONTENT OF TYPICAL ALCOHOLIC BEVERAGES

3.2 Beer	Not More Than 3.2%
"Regular" Beer	3.8% – 4%
Malt Liquor	6%
Wine Cooler	Less Than 7%, Usually 5%
Dinner Wine	10 – 12%
Fortified Wine	17 – 20%
Distilled Liquor	40 – 50%
Grain Alcohol	95%

The amount of absolute alcohol in a can of beer or a wine cooler is no less potent than the same amount of absolute alcohol when contained in an ounce of Jack Daniels. In fact, American drinkers consume as much absolute alcohol from beer as from wine and distilled spirits combined. Therefore, do not consider your teenager's consumption of beer or wine coolers as a safe and beneficial apprenticeship for the "real world" of adult social drinking. As a drinker, underage or otherwise, he or she is already a full-fledged member of a "real" social drinking world and, as such, is subject to all the associated risks.

The Effects Of Alcohol On The Body

When alcohol enters the body it acts almost immediately on the brain's central control area to depress brain activity. The initial effect is on those parts of the brain which affect *learned* behavior patterns such as self-control. As the amount of alcohol in the blood increases, vision becomes impaired, depth perception becomes distorted, and memory, muscle coordination, balance and speech become faulty. A still higher blood alcohol level depresses deeper parts of the brain, severely affecting judgment. The mind becomes unable to integrate information. Complex activity, such as driving a car, becomes extremely dangerous. Unfortunately, people who are drunk often *feel* perfectly competent.

At some point, if steady, heavy drinking continues, the alcohol anesthetizes the deepest levels of the brain and can cause coma or death by depressing heart functions and breathing. According to emergency room personnel and student "grapevines," coma and near-death of 12-18 year old alcohol users are not unusual occurrences.

How Fast Does Alcohol Take Effect?

The generally accepted way to measure the degree of intoxication is by Blood Alcohol Concentration (BAC). The rapidity with which alcohol enters the bloodstream, increases the BAC, and affects the brain and other parts of the body, depends on several factors: the person's age and personal alcohol tolerance, how fast they drink, food in the stomach, the dilution of the alcohol, their weight, medication, general health and psychological conditions.

Methods of measuring BAC include blood test, urinalysis, "breathalizer", or less directly measurable coordination tests.

A BAC chart appears in this book as part of the topic on drinking and driving. Look at it and let your teenager get an idea of how easy it is to become under the influence.

THE RELATION OF EFFECTS TO BAC	
.02%	Slightly elated, possibly impaired
.05%	Presumed 'impaired' under Colorado law
.10%	Presumed 'under the influence'
.15%	Effects of drinking obvious to everyone
.30%	Stuporous
.40%	Unconscious, possibly in a coma and on the verge of death

Alert your teenager to these facts about cause and effect. For more information, contact the Council on Alcoholism or your family physician.

Health Problems Associated With Excessive Alcohol Use

The most widely known disease attributed to alcohol is, of course, alcoholism. Evidence suggests that young people who begin using alcohol at an early age may have an increased potential for developing this unfortunate disease. The roots of alcoholism and other addictions are not totally clear, although researchers, including neuroscientists and geneticists, are examining a number of theories. The debate also continues regarding the degree to which a person's susceptibility is physical rather than psychological. Many experts agree, however, that the development of alcoholism involves interplay between biological and environmental factors.

One physiological theory which has been investigated and accepted by some experts is very logically explained and might help your teenager to better understand and respect the biological mechanics of alcoholism. Alcohol, when ingested by the *non-alcoholic,* is broken down by the liver into acetaldehyde, a toxic substance. This then breaks down into acetic acid which is eliminated from the body by the lungs, kidneys and through perspiration.

In the *alcoholic,* according to this theory, the breakdown of acetaldehyde into acetic acid is performed at half the normal rate, resulting in acetaldehyde buildup in the liver, heart muscle, and brain. Acetaldehyde in the brain interacts with the neurotransmitter, dopamine, and forms THIQ. This THIQ, found only in the brain of the alcoholic, can trigger the need for more alcohol to counter the painful effects of the progressive buildup of acetaldehyde.

Other diseases most commonly linked to alcohol are cirrhosis of the liver, chronic brain injury, heart disease, fetal alcohol syndrome, and certain types of cancer. Acute gastritis and widened blood vessels in the skin can also result. In addition to traffic deaths, other types of death attributed to alcohol abuse include overdose, suicide, fire, violent death (assault, stabbing, shooting, etc.) and exposure — especially among adolescents.

FACTS ABOUT NICOTINE

Nicotine

Nicotine, the active ingredient in tobacco, is a poisonous alkaloid extracted from tobacco as an oily, acrid liquid and used as an insecticide. Taken in its purer forms, it is almost instantly fatal to humans. Absorbed from tobacco (smoking, chewing, or snuff dipping), it raises blood pressure and negatively affects the heart and nervous system.

All-Tobacco Cigarettes

According to the National Institute on Drug Abuse, smoking is our country's largest addiction. One-third of the population is dependent on nicotine. Approximately one-fifth of the high school seniors surveyed in 1985 reported using cigarettes daily. In the last twenty years smoking has been linked to lung diseases and cancer.

Tobacco is often the first illegal and potentially dangerous substance a child tries. As a result of peer pressure, many children step over an invisible line by experimenting with tobacco in some form — usually smoking. When he or she experiences few adverse reactions from the old type "weed," it is easier to move on to other substances. Even though tobacco is not strictly a psychoactive substance, many experts feel that a significant percentage of regular adolescent tobacco users are on their way into the drug culture.

Clove Cigarettes

Indonesian clove cigarettes, also called kreteks, are marketed under exotic brand names like Gudang Garam, Kuta, Djarum and Krakatoa. Until recently, many smokers of kreteks erroneously believed they contained no tobacco and were a safe alternative to cigarette smoking.

According to the American Lung Association, clove cigarettes are composed of 60-70% tobacco and 30-40% ground cloves, clove oil and other additives. When burned, they produce higher levels of tar, nicotine, and carbon monoxide than moderate all-tobacco cigarettes. Therefore, it is suggested that clove cigarettes pose a comparable, if not greater, risk to lung health.

In the past year, there have been multiple reports of cases of shortness of breath, coughing up blood and lung infections associated with smoking these products. There is suspicion that the inhalation of some additive or toxin in the smoke of Indonesian kreteks might produce acute or fatal lung injury in circumstances where other potential causes of lung damage, such as influenza virus, are present. At least two such victims have died, although the cause-and-effect relationship has not been clearly established.

In addition to causing an allergic reaction in some people, eugenal, the active ingredient in cloves, can affect the blood pressure, hormones and muscles. Dr. Tee Guidotti, a Canadian, thinks that eugenol not only may be toxic, but also may immobilize cells that fight infection. Research has not been conclusive. Meanwhile, the state of New Mexico has outlawed clove cigarettes and some other states, including Colorado, are considering regulation of their sale and use.

Smokeless Tobacco

Madison Avenue has sold teenage America the idea that snuff and chewing tobacco are macho, safe and simple alternatives to smoking. Some researchers, however, are finding that the consequences of chewing tobacco are much more serious than those suffered from smoking it. Since 1974 sales of smokeless tobacco have been rising by 11% annually, largely because young people find it increasingly fashionable. The telltale little worn circle on a back jeans pocket where the can is tucked has become a badge of honor for some teenagers.

Regular use of a pinch of tobacco in the cheek or lower lip will, after even a few months, irritate the sensitive mucous membrane of the cheek and lower lip into laying a type of white cell callus called leukoplakia. Continued use of smokeless tobacco causes an estimated 6% of these leukoplakic lesions to insidiously develop into oral cancer. According to Adapt Insight, investigators at the National Cancer Institute have observed a fourfold increase of oral cancer among people who dip or chew. This increased risk for cancer of the cheek and gum is nearly fiftyfold among long-term chewers.

Other problems caused by smokeless tobacco are being seen regularly by the nation's dentists. Teenagers are coming in with gums detached from their teeth and with the membranes that connect the lip or the cheek to the gums just about eroded away. Many of the little dippers and chewers of the eighties can look forward to serious problems a decade from now.

If you are the parent of a smokeless tobacco user, order a reprint of "Sean Marsee's Smokeless Death" by Jack Fincher which appeared in the October, 1985 issue of *Reader's Digest*. This is the graphic account of the tragic and torturous death of an 18-year-old high school track star. The article could have a terrific impact on your young user. Orders should be sent to: Reprint Editor, *Reader's Digest*, Box 25, Pleasantville, New York 10570.

——— FACTS ABOUT MARIJUANA ———

Statistics

Alcohol may be the most frequent substance used by adolescents, but marijuana isn't far behind. Almost 1 in 20 students admitted daily marijuana use in the 1985 High School Senior Survey, and 26% reported having used it in the 30 days prior to the survey. Of the 54% who said they had tried marijuana, 41% indicated that they had used it in the last year.

Marijuana — The Drug

Marijuana (also called "pot," "grass," "Mary Jane," "reefer," "weed," and numerous other names) is the name of the crude drug made from the leaves, small stems, and flowering tops of a plant called *Cannabis sativa*. The plant grows wild and is easily cultivated throughout the world. The potency of the plant varies depending upon soil and climatic conditions. Hashish, a more potent form of marijuana, is derived from the resin scraped off leaves. The strength of marijuana now smoked in the U.S. has increased 300 times over the past several years. Marijuana currently on the streets is frequently stronger than hashish. Marijuana, most often, is smoked as a hand-rolled cigarette called a joint or in a pipe. It can also be added to food.

The level of THC, marijuana's principle psychoactive ingredient, determines the strength of the marijuana itself. Studies indicate that the THC, which is fat-soluble rather than water-soluble, clears out of the bloodstream rapidly, but is stored in the fatty tissue of the brain and reproductive organs. The derivative products of THC are flushed out of the body slowly. Depending on frequency of use and dosage, THC can be detected in the body for as long as 28 days.

The Effects Of Marijuana On The Body

Quite simply, a marijuana user feels "high" rather quickly. Possibly, they may have a pleasant hallucinatory experience coupled with a feeling of detachment from reality ("spaced out"). Following the initial euphoria, negative feelings may surface such as depression, paranoia, abnormal fears and anxiety. Marijuana produces temporary disturbances in the brain's electrical activity and disrupts the normal flow of chemical messages that transmit and process thought. This impairs short-term memory, alters the sense of time and reduces the ability to perform tasks requiring concentration, swift reaction and coordination. Physically the user's heart and pulse rate increase. Pituitary blood levels are lowered, as well as other hormones that govern sexual development.

What Is Marijuana "Burnout"?

"Burnout" is a term first used by marijuana smokers themselves to describe the effect of prolonged and heavy marijuana use. The "burned-out" teenage user, often characterized by a blank, zombie-like look, functions poorly, is almost always high and appears dull, slow moving and inattentive. Although the specific causes of "burnout" are not yet known, a combination of factors is being researched. These include examining the possibility of saturation of lipid storage areas and permanent cell destruction.

Health Problems Associated With Marijuana Use

Until recently, moderate marijuana use was considered to be no more hazardous to one's health than moderate social drinking. The results of long term use will not be known for some time, but current research indicates that there are definite dangers known and serious questions to be resolved. A major concern is marijuana's effect on the brain and its interference with psychological functioning. Another is the risk to the reproductive system.

There is definite risk to the lungs. Research shows that one marijuana joint a day decreases some lung functions as much as smoking 7-20 cigarettes. Marijuana smoke contains 50% more carcinogens than tobacco smoke. Most scientists agree that instances of pot-induced lung cancer will crop up more often as marijuana completes its second decade as a mass appeal recreational drug.

Under certain circumstances, marijuana, when combined with alcohol, may contribute to an overdose of alcohol. This adverse reaction is described at the end of this section. For a more in-depth understanding of the health problems associated with marijuana use, read *Marijuana Alert* by Peggy Mann. Other books referenced in Appendix K also contain valuable information about marijuana which is beyond the scope of this book. Keep in mind that additives to marijuana (PCP, cocaine, etc.) may cause more of a reaction than the user bargains for.

──── FACTS ABOUT COCAINE & CRACK ────

Statistics

Cocaine abuse in the United States has reached epidemic proportions. No longer uniquely the drug of the very rich and famous, it has rapidly permeated virtually every geographic area and socio-economic group — INCLUDING TEENAGE GROUPS! It is estimated that 6-8 million Americans use cocaine at least once a month and that one of every ten have tried the drug at least once.

In recent years, several states have consistently ranked high in regard to prevalence of cocaine use and abuse. This fact, coupled with the recent decrease in the cost of cocaine, renders cocaine use a potential problem among teenagers in many communities. Reportedly, the current retail price of cocaine powder is $75 to $100 per gram. "Coke-rocks," a cocaine derivative, is now available to California teenagers for $10 to $25. "Crack," or freebase rocks, is said to be available to New York City teenagers at prices ranging from $2 to $50 per vial.

One out of every six of the high school seniors surveyed in 1985 admitted to having tried cocaine at least once. Of these, 13% had used it in the last year and 7% indicated that they had used it at least once in the 30 days prior to the survey. Only .4% reported using cocaine daily. However, the current teenage crack epidemic is not reflected in these figures. Statistics for 1986 will undoubtedly be higher due to this unprecedented phenomenon.

Cocaine — The Drug

Cocaine (also known as "coke," "toot," "happy dust," etc.) is an alkaloid chemical extracted from the leaves of the coca bush, a South American shrub. The extract is refined into a water soluble white crystaline powder, which is then normally "cut" with sugars or cheaper drugs, some of which produce dangerous side effects. Cocaine, however, is available in many forms and is of varying purity. A "line" of cocaine powder (25-30 milligrams) is usually sniffed or snorted through the nostrils. Injection is the second most popular form of taking the drug. Rock cocaine is pulverized and then snorted. Smoking cocaine base using sophisticated paraphernalia ("free basing") is a less popular, very expensive and very dangerous form of absorption. Crack, a type of freebase which is becoming extremely popular, is either smoked in a pipe, or the pellets are crumbled into marijuana or tobacco for smoking. A few users even ingest cocaine orally. Others apply it to the gum or other mucous membranes.

The Effects Of Cocaine

A tiny amount of cocaine (1-3 milligrams) absorbed into the bloodstream produces profound stimulating effects on the brain by releasing the chemical norepinephrine from the nerve endings. Initially, it induces a temporary feeling of heightened energy, exhilaration, and power lasting about 20 minutes. This is associated with an increase in heart and breathing rates and elevated blood pressure. The "superperson" feeling is routinely followed in 30-60 minutes by depression and the need for more cocaine and other drugs. Not only does rapid tolerance develop with continued cocaine use, but it is also considered highly addictive.

Health Problems Associated With Cocaine Use

The frequent snorting of cocaine can irritate the nostrils, throat, and sinuses, producing sores and killing the tissue of the membranes which line the interior of the nose. Chronic snorters often suffer perforations of the septum. Heavy cocaine use may be indicated physically by cold sweats, pallor, tremors, heavy limbs, aggressive behavior, insomnia and weight loss. Psychologically, the user may experience intense anxiety, depression and confusion, hallucinations and paranoid delusions. Smoking cocaine increases the chances for serious emotional reactions. Evidence indicates that chronic abuse can also cause damage to the vocal cords, impaired eyesight, malnutrition, sexual dysfunction, and a variety of dental problems.

Sudden Death From Cocaine Use

In June of 1986, Americans were shocked by the cocaine-related deaths of two outstanding young athletes: Len Bias, an All-American basketball player from the University of Maryland, and Don Rogers, a talented defensive back for the Cleveland Browns. These tragic and widely publicized deaths serve as a dramatic example of the indisputable fact that cocaine is a killer which can randomly strike any level of user — including two of the strongest and healthiest young men in our country. Prior to the publicity surrounding these two tragedies, few people other than medical authorities were aware that cocaine can be fatal on the first dose —that first dose which is often so attractive to the curious adolescent experimenter.

Yet, federal drug abuse experts say the deaths from cocaine-related heart attacks and emergency room visits have roughly tripled since 1981. Medical examiners in several cities report a rise of more than 300%. Oddly enough, as the number of deaths and serious non-fatal medical consequences increase sharply, government figures indicate that cocaine use may be leveling off. Be aware, however, that your child is at risk so long as any form of the drug is available, affordable and attractive in any way.

Although it has been suggested that "scare tactics" and drug facts alone are not necessarily an effective deterrent to teenagers inclined to experiment with drugs, certain circumstances provide a powerful "attention-grabber" which may cause teenagers to consider more seriously the tragic consequences of one-time drug experimentation as well as more regular drug use. By what process does cocaine cause sudden death? How did Len Bias and Don Rogers die?

A July 18, 1986 article in *The Denver Post* summarized statements made by Donald Ian Macdonald, M.D., Administrator of the Alcohol, Drug Abuse and Mental Health Administration, regarding the four documented ways cocaine can kill suddenly:

- ✔ Cocaine's sudden stimulation of the central nervous system can send a person into convulsions, followed by collapse of the respiratory system.

- ✔ The drug can affect the nerves that regulate the heart beat, leading to an irregular beat called arrhythmia. The most serious arrhythmia, ventricular fibrillation, can result in cardiac arrest and almost instantaneous death.

- ✔ Cocaine stimulates the heart to beat faster and require more oxygen, while at the same time narrowing the blood vessels that carry oxygen to the heart. A section of the heart muscle can be starved of oxygen and damaged, a situation known clinically as myocardial infarction or more commonly as a heart attack.

- ✔ The same stimulated heartbeat can rapidly increase blood pressure, and the rapid increase can burst a weak blood vessel in the brain that can handle the ordinary pressure. The result is intracranial hemorrhage or a stroke.

Depending on your child's level of comprehension, the above facts may provide some excellent food for thought about the potentially fatal price of cocaine experimentation. The first experiment could well be the last!

"Crack"

In a booklet intended for parents of the adolescent, "crack," a cocaine distillate, rates a topic of its own due to its alarming popularity among teenagers. The term crack refers to the crackling sound the substance makes when it is heated. However, it is also known as "base," "baseball," "rock," "gravel," and "roxanne." Originally imported from the Bahamas around 1983, it was available first in Los Angeles and Miami, then New York City. At this writing, the drug is reportedly available in 25 states, including at least 17 major cities. The crack problem seems to be increasing at an exponential rate. Sectors of society previously not associated with cocaine use are smoking this new, powerful and relatively inexpensive form of the drug. Thus, our nation's teenagers are seriously threatened by an extremely infectious crack epidemic.

Crack is cocaine hydrochloride formed by mixing cocaine with baking soda and water. The resulting product is a paste of cocaine freebase in which the cocaine base (alkaloid) has been released from the hydrochloride ions (salt). When the paste-like substance hardens into smokable form, it is broken into small pieces or professionally pressed into dose-size pellets weighing approximately 125 milligrams. More sophisticated dealers are said to label their merchandise with brand names — "White Cloud," "Super," "Conan" and "Cloud Nine."

Physically, crack is a light brown pea-size ball or chunk, which is commonly sold in a vial containing several of these pellets or rocks. Thus, it is convenient to carry around the schoolyard for both buyer and seller. A single pellet usually costs from $10 to $20. Inexplicably, crack is sometimes less expensive than the cocaine powder necessary to produce the equivalent freebase. The effect of smoking this form of cocaine is five to ten times more powerful than "snorting" cocaine powder. Reportedly, it has the same potency as freebased cocaine without the expensive and dangerous aspects of the freebasing process which injured comedian Richard Pryor.

Thus, crack is a cheap, easily obtainable, convenient drug which packs a tremendous wallop. What could be more enticing to a vulnerable, thrill-seeking teenager? Although crack's high is immediate and very intense, it is of short duration (3-5 minutes) and is followed by crushing depression. Reportedly, this "crash" is sometimes softened with beer or "harder" alcoholic beverages. After experiencing crack once, few can resist the craving to try it again. Unfortunately crack's unprecedented "popularity" with teenagers may be also due to the fact that addiction is possible after just a few "hits" (uses), although it usually takes several weeks. At that point, repeated use is a sign of insidious craving rather than popularity.

Is crack more dangerous than any other form of cocaine? Most definitely! An article entitled "A 'Higher' Cocaine," which appeared in the April, 1986 "Prevention Parentline," a bimonthly publication of the National Federation of Parents for Drug-Free Youth, quotes Dr. Arnold M. Washton, Director of Research for the national 800-COCAINE hotline. "Crack magnifies all the cocaine-related problems we've seen to date. Inhaling purified cocaine gets the substance into the bloodstream faster (within 10 seconds) than snorting cocaine powder and at higher concentrations. It is the faster and more potent action that makes crack more addicting, more toxic, and more physically harmful. Lung damage, brain seizures and heart attacks are far more likely to occur with freebase rocks (crack)."

Dr. Washton concurs with some other medical experts and law enforcement officials that crack is more than just a slight variation of sniffable cocaine. He explains, "The high these people describe is not even comparable. It is unmatched in its euphoria and exhilaration. Clinicians need to know about it. Parents need to know about it... It's almost like we're talking about a different drug here."

Wherever crack appears, there is a startling increase in petty crime. Scores of addicts, including teenagers, are turning to stealing, prostitution and drug dealing to support their habit. The paranoia and agitation caused by a crack "high" often result in violent crime — some of which is being committed by teenagers. Many law enforcement officials seem to feel that the crack epidemic is creating a second epidemic — one of urban lawlessness.

Although crack is presently available in only half of the United States, there are already an estimated one million users. According to Dr. Washton, this number is increasing at the rate of 2,000 new users per day — many of them teenagers. Between September 1985 and May 1986, the number of cocaine users calling the national 800-COCAINE hotline with crack-related problems rose from zero percent to 33%. Crack abusers are now showing up in local emergency rooms and treatment centers in record numbers. Some enlightening statistics may soon be available. Make sure your teenager isn't one of them. Prevention is critical!

FACTS ABOUT "DESIGNER DRUGS"

"Ecstasy." "China White." Designer perfumes, perhaps? Not quite. They are street names for two of the hundreds of "designer drugs" now available to America's teenagers. Designer drugs are not considered teenage gateway drugs, nor were they mentioned per se in the results of the 1985 High School Senior Survey. However, many experts fear designer drugs may constitute the next drug epidemic, as crack has formed the current one. Like crack, they are highly addictive and very dangerous. A monster dose is the size of a pinhead, which in part explains why they are rarely detected in ordinary drug tests of body fluids. Their conceivable appeal to teenagers is that they are relatively cheap, fantastically powerful and infinitely available.

The "eighties" version of the designer drug phenomenon is already estimated to be a billion-dollar industry, although at this writing, it is still in its early stages. According to the United States Drug Enforcement Agency (DEA), these drugs are currently most visible in big cities on both coasts (particularly California) and in Texas. However, it is not limited to these areas. Reportedly, Atlanta teenagers are smoking "juice," a mixture of a designer drug and cocaine.

What then are designer drugs? How do they rate such a chic-sounding name? Designer drug is a term of reference encompassing a wide range of insidious chemical substances which straddle the fence separating legal and illegal drug classifications. Certain substances are designated by law as "Controlled Substances" and, as such, are regulated by the federal and state governments. There are several categories, or "Schedules," of controlled substances. For example, a drug, or substance, may be catagorized as legal for medical purposes and illegal for any other purpose. Another might be classified illegal for any use other than restricted research. These regulated substances are defined under law by their exact molecular structure. Circumventing this judicious procedure for identifying controlled substances is the crux of the designer drug business.

By subtly altering the chemical structure of an existing illegal drug, the underground chemist can create a variation of the drug that is not illegal. The designer drug can be manufactured, sold and used legally until scientists are able to decipher its chemical structure so that the DEA can take steps to outlaw it. When this happens, the designer/chemist simply goes back to the drawing board and comes up with another new (and legal) variation. A chart of controlled substances, their uses and effects appears in Appendix A.

A single laboratory is able to produce a phenomenal quantity of a drug and flood the market with it long before the DEA can take action. There are many of these illicit labs scattered around the country. California lawmen estimate that for each of the 235 labs they hit in 1985, three were missed. Reportedly, the underground chemist can manufacture $2 million worth of "synthetic heroin" by investing in some common lab equipment and $500 worth of chemicals. His entire operation can take place in a bathroom-size lab.

Although many of these drugs are variations of heroin and cocaine, the designer market is not limited to those particular drugs. There are known chemical patterns for scores of legal and illegal drugs, from cocaine and heroin to marijuana, LSD and Quaaludes. Experts disagree about whether designer drugs produce exactly the same effects as the parent drug. At issue is not only the similarity of effect, but also the potent and deadly consequences of the designer drugs.

Government officials refer to designer drugs by the less glamorous name of "controlled substance analogs." The DEA first encountered them in the late 1960s when STP, MDA and other hallucinogenic drugs similar to LSD appeared. Prevalent in the 1970s were chemical analogs of PCP. However, the real crisis developed in the 1980s with the creation of extremely potent synthetic heroin. Heroin analogs fall into two major categories — analogs of fentanyl (a surgical anesthetic known as Sublimaze) and analogs of meperidine (Demerol).

- ✔ Fentanyl analogues, originally sold under the name "China White," are considered to be 1,000-2,000 times more potent than heroin. When the DEA placed the drug on Schedule I as a controlled substance, designers produced at least ten other versions. Some reports indicate that the fentanyl-based drugs are linked to over 100 recent deaths.

- ✔ The less deadly meperidine analogs (MPPP) pose another very serious and potentially crippling health hazard. Unless executed under carefully controlled conditions, the synthesis of MPPP can create a by-product known as MPTP. This is a neurotoxic substance which causes an irreversible condition with the symptoms of Parkinson's disease — tremors, muscular rigidity, abnormally slow movement and speech, etc.

"Ecstasy," or MDMA, is an analog of MDA, an hallucinogen of the 1960s, and also methamphetamine, a stimulant. These analogs are synthetic cocaine-like stimulants and are particularly accessible to younger age groups. Reportedly, persons taking multiple doses of Ecstasy have experienced severe anxiety reactions, paranoia, fear, depression and insomnia. Research has demonstrated recently that Ecstasy can destroy nerve terminals in the brain. It is called "LSD of the '80s."

There are probably hundreds of designer drugs available in the United States — too many to describe in detail. Why are they considered more dangerous than their parent botanical narcotics? Usually, the danger is more acute because of their abnormally high potency. In addition, they have randomly demonstrated hazardous effects which are bizarre and unpredictable. When a teenager — or anyone else — uses designer drugs, he or she becomes a human guinea pig, who is subjected to the same risks as an experimental animal. Thus, as with crack — prevention is critical!

ADVERSE REACTIONS FROM COMBINING ALCOHOL WITH OTHER DRUGS

Adolescents should be made acutely aware of the dangers of mixing alcohol with marijuana, as well as prescription and non-prescription drugs. Alcohol and certain other drugs work in the same areas of the brain. Combinations may intensify a person's reaction to the alcohol *and* to the other drug(s), multiply the intoxicating effects and, in some cases, lead to death (including traffic deaths).

Amphetamines/Cocaine/Preludin/Caffeine — These antagonize the sedative effects of alcohol but do not improve the decreased motor functions resulting from the alcohol.

Antibiotics/Anti-infective Agents (Flagyl, Chloromycetin, etc.) — This may cause nausea, vomiting, and headache — possibly convulsions, especially those taken for urinary tract infections.

Antidepressants (Elavil, Triavil, etc.) — Certain antidepressants combined with red wines like Chianti can be lethal. Other combinations could lead to excessive sedation, incoordination, and stomach upset.

Antihistamines (Coricidin, Contac, etc.) — This interaction can produce multiplied sedation. It can dangerously decrease performance skills (driving, walking, etc), impair judgment, and reduce alertness.

Liquid Cold And Cough Remedies — Many of these contain alcohol and amphetamines. One should avoid driving, because of the potential drowsiness.

Marijuana — This combination, fairly common among teenagers, is more hazardous *and* more intoxicating than the use of either by itself. One joint plus one beer produces the intoxicating effects of multiple beers. Controlled road tests have shown that this combination makes driving extremely hazardous, even though the BAC may remain within the legal limit. Remember, too, that THC can remain in the system for several weeks.

The THC in marijuana turns off the gag reflex in the brain and, thus, suppresses the feeling of nausea that may accompany drunkenness. As a result, large quantities of alcohol can be consumed quickly. This may cause acute alcohol poisoning and lead to sudden death.

Painkillers (Codeine, Darvon, Narcotics, etc.) — Analgesics plus alcohol increase nervous-system depression and multiply the sedative effect, making driving dangerous. Respiratory arrest and death can result.

Sedatives/Tranquilizers/Sleeping Pills/Barbituates (Dalmane, Quaaludes, Valium, etc.) — Any of these plus alcohol produce an increased sedative effect that will dangerously interfere with coordination, concentration, and judgment. The combination can be fatal.

Time Release Capsules — Often, alcohol quickly dissolves the outer covering of "tiny time pills." Thus, an 8-12 hour dose of medication may be released all at once, causing toxic effects, multiplied sedation, etc.

3. The Teen Social Scene

"HANGIN' OUT" AND OTHER SOCIAL "HAPPENINGS"

As you read in a previous section, adolescents are fiercely attached to their peer group. They want to be free to mingle with "the crowd" — without the intervention of adults — as much as is humanly possible. When kids are unsupervised and have no particular objective in mind other than being together and socializing, it is known as "hangin' out." Hanging out is not a new phenomenon by any means. As teenagers, we who are now parents did some "hangin' out" ourselves — undoubtedly for the same reasons our own children are doing it. But the logistics of where and how seem to have changed markedly.

Today's teenagers live in a world of big shopping malls, convenience stores and fast food chains. Our fondly remembered teenage hangouts (the hamburger joints, root beer stands and soda shops) have disappeared into the corporate structure. "Cruisin' " the main drag all night is often out; gas costs too much. Other than teen clubs and sports centers, there are few, if any, commercial establishments where teens are solicited or even welcomed for an *entire evening*. A $5.00 first run movie lasts 1½ to 2 hours . . . after that what? Where do our teenagers go these days just to hang out together?

Teenagers in every community have their customary hangouts and social policies. However, for many of them, drugs — including alcohol — are a determining factor in their social choices. Let's take a look at some of the alternatives potentially available for "hangin' out."

Shopping Malls, Theaters, Arcades, Amusement Parks, Etc.

Younger teenagers go to the malls, etc. to have a good time. In these public settings, they feel free to meet their friends, shop, be entertained, check out other kids, meet students from other schools and so on. It's entertainment at its least expensive best.

There are, however, a handful of kids who have other motives. They drink in their cars, smoke marijuana outside (more so when it's dark) and then come inside. Inside the mall they do the following:

- ✔ Are rowdy, cause fights, harass customers, and pick on anyone they so choose.
- ✔ Store drugs in the lockers near the restrooms, make a "deal" in the mall and then give the locker key to the purchaser.
- ✔ Exchange drugs and money in the restrooms.
- ✔ Shop lift, often on dares from their friends.

Make sure your young teenager is aware of these pitfalls, so that he or she doesn't inadvertently become a victim.

Convenience Stores and Parking Lots

In a number of high school communities where there is a centrally located convenience store with a reasonably large parking lot, activity-hungry teenagers press it into service as "the" hangout location. In areas without such attractively situated convenience stores, there are usually other readily accessible business locations with tolerably well-lighted parking areas — grocery stores, fast food places, even cycle shops — which serve the same purpose. However, the convenience store offers some unique possibilities as well as the more standard ones.

It is the officially appointed meeting place and central information point. Teenagers congregate to discuss who's doing what, to share party possibilities, or to just hook-up with someone — anyone — for the evening. If there is no party or other interesting activity, then the convenience store itself may be arbitrarily designated as the party *and* the activity. So far this description is somewhat reminiscent of the drive-in restaurants which existed "back in the old days."

However, unlike yesteryear, few businesses today are operated primarily for teen hangin' out. On a dull evening, when the convenience store seems to be the only game in town, a mob of teenagers looking for excitement and a good time can quite unintentionally make a nuisance and a menace of themselves for the store's customers and employees. A relative minority of teenagers warrant far more serious complaints including shoplifting, vandalism and fights or assaults. The police are called on nights such as these — usually more than once. Periodically, teenagers are also arrested at convenience stores on charges of illegal possession, procuring for a minor, and criminal trespass. These arrests are precipitated by underage teenagers drinking and carousing in the parking lot.

There are numerous convenience store customers over the legal drinking age. Many of them — and not necessarily just young people — are agreeable to accepting money from a minor (some as young as 12) and to purchasing beer for that minor and his/her friends. (The same is often true outside liquor stores.) The clerks and managers usually require proper ID and keep a sharp lookout for suspicious purchases, but it is impossible on a busy night to effectively control the final destination of every can of beer that leaves the store.

The younger teenagers, who don't yet have transportation, also hang out at the local convenience store: observing, getting a ride from upper-classmen, conning beer from strangers, and sometimes getting into trouble. Thus, by the time they reach "cruisin' age," they are old hands at "Convenience Club" activities.

Fast Food Chains, Sports Centers, Teen Clubs

Most teenagers feel that fast food chains are not conducive to hanging out. Eat and leave just isn't the name of the hangout game. Nor are these establishments, understandably, particularly hospitable to large groups of teenagers. The managers undoubtedly feel that normal teenage exuberance, which can easily get out of control, will drive away the more affluent adult customers. They may also be wary of property damage, vindictive or otherwise, which has been reported by some such places. The establishments which feature things to do, such as video games, seem slightly more hospitable to a few reasonably well-behaved teenagers hanging out with a specific purpose in mind.

The manager of one bowling center, which is located next to a large high school, stated that although they have a junior bowling league, they do not encourage teens who are not accompanied by parents to hang out there due to the potential for "horseplay." If they consider a teen rowdy, or if too many teens congregate in the bowling areas or in the video and pool rooms, the management either calls the parents or police. Despite its close proximity to the high school, a teenager who just wants to "shoot the breeze" for awhile is not welcome.

On the other side of the fence, the teen clubs which are flourishing in some metropolitan areas welcome teenagers with open arms. We interviewed an owner of Norman's Teen Club which counts many of Eastern Colorado's 13-18 (average age 15) year olds among its customers. Currently, for $3.50 plus the price of soft drinks, a teen can buy an evening of music and dancing from 7 p.m. to 11-11:30 p.m. three to four nights a week. This particular club, which can hold up to 900, has the atmosphere of a night club. Teenagers are checked at the door for possession of alcohol/drugs, and any found is confiscated. A teenager who is judged to be under the influence is taken to the office and given a choice of the manager calling either his or her parents or the police. Eight security people (bouncers) and one uniformed police officer are responsible for maintaining order inside the club.

According to the management, security personnel also periodically patrol the parking lot and check for teenagers loitering and/or drinking in cars. Offenders are asked to leave or they are ticketed. Rumors abound about alleged incidents at various teen clubs or in the club parking lots. To verify their authenticity, concerned parents should call their local police department. If a teen club exists in your area, feel free to call the management of the club and possibly go over and see the facility. Most teen clubs welcome parental inquiries and/or check-out visits.

Parks, Recreation Areas, Formally Named Fields

In Southeast Denver, when the weather is nice, teenagers consider the "Res," better known as the Cherry Creek Reservoir, the place to be. There the kids swim, water ski, play touch football, etc., or just hang out. It is also a popular location for teen beer parties, some of which are in conjunction with other activities. Every community's teenagers seem to have their own version of the "Res." In an area of Southern Michigan, it's the "other side" of Lake Success. In Gage, Oklahoma, it's the "Gage Beach," an artesian well on the outskirts of town. From the city parks of Millburn, New Jersey to the fig orchards of Fresno, California, gregarious teenagers manage to appropriate their own particular outdoor areas for recreational hangin' out.

Another favorite hangout site for the high schoolers, when the police start cracking down at the convenience stores and other favorite parking lots, is the remote deserted field. Some of these have been fondly named by their young patrons and are regular hangouts during good weather. An informal poll of teenagers in several states netted some very creative names for these beloved pieces of undeveloped real estate: "The Outlet," "The Dodge," "The Grass," "The Drain" are but a few. As one high school senior put it, "'The Outlet' is a place for us to escape from the hassle of cops and be with our friends." The scene here is usually the same as elsewhere — a lot of socializing, a little bit (or, at times, a lot) of beer, and when the wrong group shows up on occasion, a "heap of trouble."

Schoolgrounds, Construction Sites, Anonymous Fields, Etc.

These hangout places are usually frequented more by young teenagers from the middle schools who don't have ready access to transportation. There are times, however, when the police have chased the upper-classmen out of every available alternative hangout/party site, and they, too, must resort to the school parking lots, roofs, playgrounds and other less public sites. The middle schoolers tell us, that, most often, their purpose in such hanging out is not only to socialize but also to do some drinking and perhaps experiment with pot. This is verified by the large number of empty beer cans and other evidence found in these areas after a particularly active weekend.

Homes Where Parents Are Absent

This is just asking for trouble whether your child is a toddler or a teen. One of the basic criteria for a "cool" hangout place is the degree of freedom it offers. As a result, nothing is quite so inviting to the teenagers (those you know and those you've never heard of) as a home, without parents, where they can hang out together. This allows them the complete freedom to do what they want, confident that their parents will NEVER find out. And experimenting with, using and even abusing alcohol and/or other drugs is often part of the game plan. Even if it isn't on the original agenda for the young teenagers, it can easily become a part of the plan when someone unexpectedly drops in with booze or marijuana. For the older teenager, absent parents may be spelled BYOB or keg party.

Reportedly, small lunch-break and after-school pot or BYOB parties are not an infrequent occurrence at students' homes where parents are regularly absent during the day — either at work or on out-of-town business trips. Working parents, once they are aware of the teen social possibilities their absence creates, might set up their own neighborhood watch to safeguard against such parties in their home. Parents who are out of town, even for a one night business trip, should make some arrangements for the supervision of their teenagers while they are gone.

Chaperoned Homes and Parties

The presence of parent(s) and/or chaperone(s) by no means insures that alcohol will not be available to underage teens. Some parents are actually unaware that a beer keg is concealed behind the bushes in the backyard. Others willingly purchase and serve alcohol for teenage parties and gatherings. Several parentally supervised 16th or 18th birthday parties and other social gatherings have gotten out of hand with very serious, even fatal, repercussions. If you want to be sure there is going to be no alcohol served or brought in, you had better call and ask. You might also ask the party-giving parents if they are aware of the tremendous legal liability they are risking.

Sleeping Over

The marathon of hanging out activities is sleeping over — what we called slumber parties. Many are exactly as we remember them from our own youth. They haven't changed in that nobody expects or gets much sleep. But they are different in that this generation's moms and dads are often not at home for the night or weekend, and in that the guest lists are sometimes coed and very flexible. For example, sophomore brother is babysitting freshman sister for the weekend. He invites his buddies to sleep over; she asks her girlfriends to do the same. A BYOB or keg party may highlight the evening, and as everyone gets wasted, they, too, decide to become sleep-over guests.

Another type of sleep-over party is what we call the "phantom sleep-over." All the kids tell their parents they are sleeping over at someone else's house, usually someone their parents don't know well — if at all. They then are free to party and/or tear around all night on their own, finally, "crashing" wherever they happen to land. If they should totally disappear, as many teenagers have in recent years, who's to know for quite some time?

Hotel/Motel Parties

These are, most often, relatively small, unchaperoned, "invitation only" parties, which take place following a special event such as prom, graduation or homecoming. There may be one host/hostess or several, who rent the room and issue invitations. There are, of course, "crashers" and party hoppers who, on a special occasion, hit every party in every hotel in town. It may be a BYOB party or the partygiver(s) may provide booze, food, or whatever. Champagne or hard liquor is usually the preferred drink. But consider: Nothing can go on in a hotel that can't also go on in a private home when parents are away for the weekend. Just be aware of what a wide social latitude our teens have available to them — *if* they have the money to spend.

What Kids Have To Say About "Hanging Out"

When interviewed about "hanging out," several teenagers agreed that probably five out of six adults have conveniently forgotten what they themselves were like as teenagers: their need for socialization, the social problems they faced, and their less acceptable social activities and pranks. These teens feel that today's adults are too prone to automatically stereotype *all* teenagers as vandals, irresponsible "hell-raisers," and worse. While acknowledging such teen types do exist, they say this sort represents a minority of the teenagers in America.

The teenagers interviewed also pointed out that many adults (including some parents) make little effort to understand today's teen: where they are coming from, where they are going and why. Rather, they tend to discount them as "non-persons" who are too much trouble to have around. These particular teens felt that since many teenagers (rightly or wrongly) see adults as disinterested, inhospitable, intolerant, or unwilling to compromise in any way, a high percentage of teenagers prefer to "do their own thing" without the interference of *any* adults. As one high school senior put it, "My Dad literally wants me to get a crewcut and do things exactly like he *thinks* he did them 30 years ago. He refuses to understand that the good old U.S. of A. in 1987, is very different for a teenager (or anyone else) than it was in 1957."

"KEG PARTIES" AND OTHER BEER BUSTS

Once upon a time, somewhere in these United States, a sophisticated teenage entrepreneur invented the "keg party," a wild and crazy, money-making free-for-all which might also have been unimaginatively dubbed "a commercial beer blast." The idea caught on and quickly spread to numerous communities around the country. Today, in many areas, keg parties are a standard, very popular, and often very dangerous part of the teenage social scene. Although teenagers in some regions of the country where this phenomenon has appeared continue to call it a "keg party," teens in some other participating locales refer to these commercial shindigs as "keggers," "beer bashers" or other definitive monikers. However, a "keg party" by any other name is still a "keg party." And it can be dynamite!

Once the word gets out about a keg party, there is absolutely no foolproof control over who is coming or how many or what will happen. Several in Colorado have erupted into violence and/or led to the deaths of several teenagers. There have been incidents of serious injuries sustained in fights, fatal and near fatal stabbings, alcohol overdose, drunk driving accidents, et cetera — all related to keg parties or other types of beer parties. Absentee parents of the kegger host have, in some cases, returned home to discover personal possessions missing (e.g., jewelry) and/or expensive property damage to their homes and grounds. Sometimes parents, often with the best of intentions, purchase the alcohol and supervise the bash. Even then, the situation often gets out of control.

What Is A Keg Party And Why?

Keg parties don't necessarily follow an exact pattern. Some are relatively tame, with as few as 50 local high school students, no fights, no drugs and no vandalism. Others might draw as many as 400 teenagers from many different areas, some of whom might carry weapons and/or have hard drugs such as "crack" or powdered cocaine for sale. The scenario created below is a fairly middle-of-the-road keg party which might typically be thrown by an ordinary teenager — yours, for example.

Several hundred photocopied fliers like this might be distributed to advertise the keg party described in the scenario.

THE KEGGER SCENARIO

Party planning

- Two 18-year-olds need money and decide to have a "kegger."

- They locate a third partner whose parents will be away for the weekend and offer to split the profits three ways if he will allow them to use his parents' home for the party. The 16 year old partner agrees.

- The three kids, all high school students, advertise the party by distributing fliers at school and outside several convenience stores. Word of the party indirectly reaches students at other high schools in town.

- On the night of the party, both 18-year-olds pick up several kegs at a liquor store, leave a deposit and pay cash for the kegs.

- At the door, guests (?) are charged $3 to drink and $1 if they aren't going to drink. The $3 people are stamped accordingly.

Party in progress

- 150 teenagers (age 15-18) pay their admission to attend the party.

    Several kids bring their own Jack Daniels which they intend to drink and share with close friends.

    One student brings a large amount of pot, which she intends to sell.

- At 12:30 AM, students from a rival school arrive and there is a disturbance.

    A fight breaks out between two boys. Several students make a futile attempt to break it up.

    In the general confusion, some contents of the dwelling are damaged or destroyed. The damage is later estimated at $2,000.

- Neighbors call the police to the scene.

50 | KIDS, DRUGS, & ALCOHOL

PARTY PARTY PARTY PARTY
2200 Blazer Trail
May 13, 7:00 PM to ???
$3.00 Admission at door
All You CAN DRINK
5 Kegs

Situation as encountered by the police

- Numerous teenagers are in varying states of intoxication:

    On the public sidewalk in front of the dwelling,

    In the yard of the dwelling,

    In the dwelling itself.

- Both of the boys involved in the fight are injured.
- Several students are passed out, apparently from alcohol overdose.
- Alcohol is in evidence, as well as the odor of pot.
- Many of the teenagers will obviously not be sober enough to drive for several hours.

Had the above party not gotten out of control, necessitating certain operating expenses (e.g., fines, legal fees, damages, etc.), our three young entrepreneurs would probably have realized a healthy profit. In part, it is this "easy money" that motivates many teenagers to throw keggers so regularly.

In some cases, however, throwing keg parties is a highly organized business. A group of high school students in Colorado which called itself "The Wrecking Crew" even opened a bank account to stash the profits from their illegal and highly lucrative enterprise. Some adults also throw keg parties which teenagers attend. Usually, but not always, this is just a quick means of raising cash for the overdue rent or car payment. A Denver woman reportedly made $1,500 from a single kegger. At the other extreme are the parents who want to have a special party for their teenager and think charging a dollar or two at the door for beer is the most economical way to cover costs.

Comments on Teenage BYOB (Bring Your Own Beer) Parties

There seem to be some parents in almost every community who say that kids are going to drink, no matter what. They feel it's better for the teenagers to drink in a supervised setting rather than doing it on the sly in a more raucous atmosphere. Thus, these parents generously provide such a setting. A student from an affluent New Jersey community described BYOB parties which are thrown by one of several "regular" party hosts every three to four weeks. The parents are usually present, and, in some cases, a security guard is hired as a bouncer. Teenagers in several locales ranging from affluent to solid middle class reported this type of beer party being organized and chaperoned by parents.

According to a number of teenagers, however, the well-intentioned, parentally supervised beer party can't compete with the impromptu bashes which befall the homes of parents who leave town and put their social-minded teenager in charge. It may start out to be "a few friends," but as the word spreads — which it inevitably seems to do — scores of kids start arriving on the scene. The final count may be one to two hundred. In many communities around the country, these informal beer blasts are a regular part of the weekend teen social scene.

Although private homes, condos, apartments and neighborhood clubhouses are often used for BYOB parties, other sites are also popular. For example, a high school student in New Mexico surreptitiously unlocked his Dad's feed store on numerous Saturday nights to provide a place for convivial teenage BYOBs. A teenager in another state managed to gain weekend access to a luxurious vacant house, complete with functioning indoor swimming pool, which he regularly used for teenage BYOB parties. Regardless of the location, it usually adds up to a mob of kids getting together to drink beer —or whatever — and have a good time.

The parents of many of these kids say they chugged a few beers themselves when they were in high school. So what's wrong with it, other than the fact that it's usually illegal? Perhaps Mom and Dad should ask themselves what percentage of the country's problem drinkers back then were between the ages of 12 and 19. By high school graduation, how many of their teenage beer drinking cronies had progressed from beer into regular use of other drugs such as marijuana and cocaine? Were colossal beer busts every weekend the exception to the teenage social norm of their day, or were such parties the only acceptable social norm available? Now ask your kids the same questions.

Even though the beer, more costly when purchased by the can or six pack, may not be flowing quite so freely, many of the problems created by keg parties also arise at BYOB parties. A potpourri of kids and booze are a volatile combination no matter what form of alcohol is available. A teenager mellowed out by a few beers might be strongly tempted to try some marijuana or crack if it's offered, although he or she would never consider it under normal circumstances. A pleasant buzz could also result in a teenager switching from a "quarters" beer game to a more lethal one played with 90 proof liquor. Will the teenager drive home after drinking, smoking marijuana or both? Obviously, the potential risks are infinite.

What Do The Police Do When They Arrive To "Bust" A Keg or BYOB Party?

Law enforcement procedures and attitudes regarding teen keg and BYOB parties vary from jurisdiction to jurisdiction. Some officers issue several warnings before taking action to disperse the party. Others clear out the party location immediately without even pausing for an explanation. When the police are called to the scene of a keg or BYOB party such as the one described in the scenario, officers usually want to restore order and eliminate the potential of violence, vandalism, injuries or drunk driving. They will, generally attempt to identify the person(s) who are responsible for the party. Officers don't want to take large numbers of people into custody, but they will do so if necessary. The following steps may be taken:

- ✔ Locate and get appropriate care for anyone who is injured, sick, or so drunk as to be a danger to themselves or others.
- ✔ Investigate any injuries or damages and locate those responsible.
- ✔ Investigate the party itself for violations and locate those responsible.
- ✔ Restore order and quiet to the area/neighborhood.

Unfortunately, when the police have had numerous citizen complaints about a teen beer party, a high priority may be to get the kids off the premises and out of the neighborhood as quickly as possible. Most often, they have no reasonable alternative.

Why Do Our Kids Go To "Keggers" And Other Beer Parties?

Whatever the reason, many of our teenagers (drinkers *and* non-drinkers) seem determined to be in on the scene regardless of the dangers involved. A group of high school students met with a concerned parent following a beer party at which a good friend had suffered respiratory arrest (stopped breathing) as the result of a .385 BAC coupled with internal injuries. The students were asked why they planned to continue to support and encourage drinking parties when they had witnessed first hand the tragedy that could result.

They analyzed it and came up with the following reasons:

- All the kids are doing it.

- They have been doing it since middle school so it has just become a "way of life" for them.

- There is nothing else to do that *everybody* likes to do and can afford.

- They enjoy drinking with their friends and they don't really *want* to stop. Some of the parties are "pretty fun" and fairly tame.

- School is big and busy. Beer parties are the only chance to meet people they want to get to know.

- They were going to make an informal pledge to watch each other in the future — "sort of a buddy system" — so something like this couldn't happen again.

It was painfully obvious that these normally intelligent teenagers felt that they themselves were immune from tragedy and uniquely different from their friend who almost died. Although the kids were all visibly shaken 24 hours after the incident, the near tragedy was all but forgotten a few weeks later, as was the "buddy system."

What Legal Liability Is Involved In "Keg And BYOB Parties?"

H. Michael Steinberg, a deputy district attorney in Arapahoe County, Colorado, has prepared Appendix G, a summary of potential charges available to the district attorney's office, based on the fact pattern presented in the "keg party scenario." This includes charges which may be brought against parents, party planners, and teenage attendees both over and under 18 relating to the alcohol. Other potential charges relate to the fight, the property damage, the marijuana, and the Jack Daniels. Crimes which could also potentially occur in a situation of this type are criminal trespass, resisting arrest, obstructing a police officer, refusing to aid a police officer and harassment. Discuss Appendix G with your teenager. It often hits home! Even though it references Colorado law, the potential charges in your state are probably similar. Your municipal or county prosecutor's office can provide this information.

Are parents held legally liable for the negligent acts of their teenage partiers? In most states the following factors are among those considered when determining parents' liability: Is the child under 18, not married or emancipated? Does the child live with his or her parents? Is the parent guilty of "negligent entrustment"? For example: Seventeen year old Jack's parents go out of town for a weekend leaving him alone and in charge of their house. They are aware that in the past six months, he has thrown a keg party each time they have left town. Neighbors have informed them that Jack's teenage guests habitually become intoxicated and violent towards one another. The parents, having discovered no damage to their home as a result of these parties, choose to ignore them. By a "reasonable person's standard," should these parents know their son will throw a dangerous and illegal kegger on any weekend they leave town, even though he does not specifically tell them of his plan?

Suppose one of the following incidents occurred at a teenage beer party: A teenage guest drives away intoxicated and causes an automobile accident which results in death and serious injury. One inebriated guest assaults another guest. The victim subsequently loses an eye as a result of the fight. A guest overdoses on alcohol taken from the parents' liquor cabinet and dies of alcohol poisoning.

The parents of the party host are subject to civil liability if it can be proven that they knew or should have known of their child's party. Further, if they gave explicit permission for the party, helped plan it and purchased the alcohol, they become entangled in criminal liability as well. Possible charges range from contributing to the delinquency of a minor to accessory to vehicular homicide. In some states, a parent may be liable for the negligent acts of their child if they themselves are negligent in failing to exercise proper control or supervision over their child, with knowledge that injury to another is a possible consequence of the child's conduct. Thus, the victim's survivors might file a civil suit against parents who had no knowledge of their teenager's party. Even if the parents were found not liable, the lawsuit could result in very costly legal fees which might exceed liability coverage.

An imaginative attorney for the plaintiff can structure a cause of action which could subject parents to phenomenal damages —actual, as well as punitive. Damages and injuries awarded in cases of this type are usually covered by the parents' homeowners liability policy up to the policy limits, which are generally $100,000. However, liability insurance does not cover punitive damages, nor does it pay for actual damages and injuries over the amount of the liability limits (e.g., $100,000). Such excess judgments must be satisfied by personal assets.

Under a theory of negligence known as *"host liability,"* juries have awarded damages far in excess of $100,000 against hosts who serve alcohol to a guest who becomes intoxicated and causes death or injury as a result of his or her intoxication. You might ask yourself how a parent qualifies as "host" in this case. In some states, if parents are found guilty of violating "duty of care," they may be held responsible for damages whether or not they knew about the child's intentional act that caused damage to others. In this case, state laws limit parental liability to a certain amount.

What Can Parents Do About The Kegger And BYOB Problem?

The Overland Community Task Force Coordinating Council in Aurora, Colorado, has held numerous meetings at which parents have expressed deep concern and frustration about the teenage kegger/beer party scene in the community and the many near tragedies which have resulted. Yet, a clear cut answer as to what parents can do about it has never emerged. Suggestions have ranged from urging the police to charge and arrest every kegger participant they can get their hands on, to holding beer parties with heavy parental supervision.

Here are a few suggestions that you might use to start the ball rolling in your own mind:

- ✔ State your position clearly! Let your teenager know exactly how you feel about teenagers drinking alcohol in *your* home and on *your* property and why. Discuss with him or her the parent/community contract in Appendix I.

- ✔ Do *not* go out of town and leave your teenager(s) *unsupervised*. Hire a responsible person with *excellent* references or swap weekends with another concerned and responsible parent. It is not fair for you to put your teenager in a position where he or she can be pressured into providing your home as a keg or beer party location — no matter how much the youngster deserves your *trust*.

✓ Emphasize your teenager's personal ownership interest in the family home and property. Encourage respect for the *value* of not only family property but public and other private property as well. This may throw a different perspective on the destructive aspects of big beer blasts.

✓ Maintain open and straightforward communication with your teenager about the current party scene. Discuss the criminal and civil liabilities associated with it and how they might affect him or her.

✓ Don't discount the problem because you feel your teenager would *never* throw or attend a beer party or kegger. Maybe he or she won't; but any teenager in a temporary financial bind might be tempted to host a keg party. Likewise, if that's where everyone is, your teenager may be tempted to drop in just "to see who's there."

✓ Let's face facts! Despite all good intentions, teenagers may still find themselves and/or their friends in a difficult situation — possibly even a potentially life-threatening one. Teach your teenager how to recognize such a situation. Urge your teenager and the friends he or she is with to call you at *any* time they need help personally or needs help for a friend. Such a call, on several occasions, has saved a child from death by *toxic alcohol overdose*.

✓ As a citizen, work with the police to help them stop keggers before they start or get out of control. Let them know about upcoming keggers or those that are in progress. Most police departments will keep such reports confidential. In that way, you have invited the police to the party so they can keep an eye on it for disturbances, drunk driving in the immediate area and underage participants.

✓ Ask your high school to assist on the keg and beer party problem. When word leaks out about an upcoming party, some school officials notify the police, who take "pre-party" action. A police officer contacts the owners of the property to find out if they are aware of the party. If they are, he informs them of the potential illegal aspects of such a party.

Encourage parent groups to assist in enhancing public awareness about the problem as it exists in your community.

For example: Put together a panel discussion for presentation to high school students and their parents which explains the criminal, civil, and insurance liability of keg and beer parties and the subsequent drinking and driving. A police officer, a judge, a municipal or county prosecutor, a civil attorney, an insurance company representative and a paramedic might be asked to serve on the panel. Ask some students to write up a typical "kegger/BYOB scenario."

✔ Get your state legislature involved in the problem. Illinois has passed a law that carries a maximum fine of $500 when it can be proved that parents had knowledge of underage drinking on the premises.

✔ Finally, keggers and other types of beer parties must satisfy some teenage need or they wouldn't occur. Non-drinkers also attend, so the need can't be *just* to drink beer. Find out what your teenager's social needs are and actively support and promote alternative social activities which will, *from his or her point of view*, satisfactorily fulfill some of those needs.

TEENAGE DRINKING AND DRIVING

The Teen Drunk Driving Problem

One of the major concerns regarding keggers and BYOB parties is the teenage drunk driving that too often follows such affairs. For example, a teenager, who is sincerely trying to be a responsible drinker (conveniently disregarding the fact that he is under legal age), may inadvertently exceed his limit. He decides to stop drinking and wait to leave the party until he is sober enough to drive. But, unlike the usual adult cocktail party, a teenage party can be ended abruptly at any time by a police "bust," which may put our partially conscientious teenager on the street — drunk.

Whether or not the officers/deputies breaking up a teen drinking party risk allowing teens who are "impaired" or "under the influence" to drive away in that condition depends upon several factors. These include the personal attitude of the lawmen on the scene, the availability of personnel, the circumstances and logistics of the particular situation, other police priorities in the city at the time, and the availability of necessary resources for viable alternatives.

In a "bust" situation, the Arapahoe County, Colorado Sheriff's Department, on occasion, has set up road blocks in the area to snare intoxicated teen drivers who are leaving a party. On the other hand, a member of another county's law enforcement agency defended his department's laxness to the *Rocky Mountain News*. In response to criticism of deputies breaking up a party and sending the young partygoers off in their cars — risking accidents, he said, "Everyone thinks it's the law enforcement's responsibility to control their children. They're saying, 'Why don't you do something with that child?', when the responsibility lies with the parents."

Teen drinking isn't limited to parties. Teenagers may drink alone or with a few friends. Some kids drink to get drunk and will be in that condition no matter when or how they hit the streets. Others get drunk by "slamming" in a drinking contest or as a result of losing at games like "quarters" or "beer pong." Whatever the reason for drinking, thousands of teenagers kill themselves or someone else each year by driving after drinking.

The Teen Impaired Driving Problem

A teenage driver is relatively inexperienced at best. Controlled road tests indicate even a slight amount of alcohol causes a deterioration of between 25 and 30 percent in driving performance of *expert* drivers. Laboratory tests on various timesharing components of driving skills such as visual search-and-recognition, tracking, and reaction time, show similar significant impairment at levels below the .05 Blood Alcohol Concentration (BAC) which, in several states, defines a legally impaired driver.

In addition, inattention and drowsiness which result from the depressant action of alcohol may lead to insufficient response in a driving emergency. The disinhibitory effects of alcohol may also cause a driver to take more risks, such as driving too fast, and to be less cognizant of the need for caution and self-restraint.

Statistical analyses have shown that while drunk drivers take their toll, the majority of alcohol-related fatal accidents are caused by drivers who are close to or under the illegal BAC. Even a little drinking affects drivers. If your teenager tells you, "I only had a couple of beers," don't be lulled into complacency. Any drinking driver is potentially dangerous!

Marijuana also affects a wide range of skills necessary for safe driving. Research shows that these skills are impaired for at least 4-6 hours after smoking a single joint. Cocaine-related automobile accidents have also been reported. Drugged driving is now under the DUI statutes of several states. The multiplier effect of combining alcohol with other drugs, such as marijuana, should be reiterated here. Controlled road tests have shown that this combination makes driving extremely hazardous, even though the BAC may remain within the legal limit.

Statistics

Youthful drivers (age 16-24) in this country make up only 17-19% of all licensed drivers. Yet, they account for a much larger percentage of all crashes, all fatal crashes and all injury accidents. In 1985, it is estimated that almost 44,000 people died and another 4 or 5 million were injured in motor vehicle accidents — about half of those fatal accidents were alcohol related. Statistics show that teenagers suffer the greatest per capita losses. The leading single cause of death among 14-15 year olds is drunk driving.

Fortunately, however, recent public awareness campaigns have contributed to a significant decrease in alcohol-related traffic deaths. According to the latest figures available, nine American teenagers die every day in alcohol related accidents. This is down from 14 per day in 1983, and new figures are expected to be even lower. Reportedly the 20 states which have raised their drinking ages since 1984 have averaged a 13% reduction in fatal traffic accidents among the 18-20 age group. However, despite the decrease, your teenager is still very much at risk.

The Criminal, Civil And Insurance Liabilities

While the cost in terms of grief, human suffering and shattered lives is incalculable, the reckonable economic and legal impact of the drunk driving problem can be absolutely staggering. Legislation regarding drinking and driving is done at the state level. Therefore, no uniform set of laws and penalties can be referenced in this section. Colorado drunk driving penalties are used merely as an example and differ somewhat from those in each of the 49 other states. Call your county or municipal prosecutor's office to find out about the specific penalties and illegal BACs in your own state.

DUI — Under Colorado law enforcement procedures for example, a teenager under 18 who is stopped on suspicion of drunk driving and is unable to perform the roadside maneuvers will be taken into custody and given a chemical breath or blood test. If the teenager's BAC is over the legal limit, he or she is charged and and put into a holding cell until released into parental custody. At that point, the teenage drunk driver is probably most concerned about loss of license and what Mom and Dad are going to say. However, there are other consequences to be considered. For example, in Colorado, the teenager, if convicted, also should expect to make as many as four court appearances, spend at least 48 hours doing community service and attend eight or so alcohol education classes of two hours each. Most likely, none of the required locations will be within easy walking distance of home or school.

The entire experience could cost around $1,000: $500 or more for an attorney, almost $300 for court costs, at least $100 for the fine, about $160 for alcohol education plus a vehicle towing charge if applicable. When the teenager's license is reinstated, he or she should be prepared for another financial jolt in the form of sky-rocketing car insurance rates, which will continue for five to seven years. Appendix H, provided by the Western Insurance Information Service, gives a very readable in-depth analysis of the automobile insurance aspects of a DUI.

Vehicular Homicide and Vehicular Assault — Yet, despite all of the consequences outlined above, the drinking teenage driver who is stopped by the law is much more fortunate than the one who is stopped by a crash. Particularly if it results in serious injuries or death. Recently, an Aurora, Colorado teenager — whom we'll call Joey — pleaded guilty to vehicular homicide and was sentenced to four years in prison for killing a woman in an alcohol-related crash. On the fatal night, which occurred three months after Joey's high school graduation, he was driving his parents' car without permission, despite the fact that his license had been suspended. His BAC was .139 from having drunk "four to five" beers in less than two hours. Disoriented by the alcohol, Joey thought he had sideswiped a metal guardrail rather than another vehicle, and did not stop.

As a result of the vehicular homicide charge, Joey, then 18, faced up to an eight-year sentence, which could have been doubled to 16 years if the judge had found aggravating circumstances. The maximum fine for this offense in Colorado is $500,000. Had Joey's victim been injured seriously rather than killed, he undoubtedly would have been charged with vehicular assault which, upon conviction, can result in a prison sentence of up to four years and a fine of up to $100,000. In return for Joey's guilty plea, prosecutors dropped additional charges of hit-and-run and driving while his license was suspended. Even though Joey did not get the maximum sentence, he still paid a substantial price for his six pack of beer. However, he recognizes that it was negligible compared to the one paid by his victim and her surviving children.

Civil Suits — In automobile accidents involving injury or death, a civil suit is very often filed against the parents of a teenage driver as well as the driver. Juries across the country are awarding millions of dollars in cases like this for loss of enjoyment of life, pain and suffering and future wage loss as the result of an accident. Most drivers have liability coverage under their auto insurance policy which would take care of the liability costs up to the liability limit of the policy. However, liability insurance does not cover punitive damages — money awarded by a jury beyond actual loss as punishment for irresponsible actions. If there were punitive damages awarded, or if the actual damages awarded against the teenager and/or his family were greater than their coverage, personal assets are seizable. This could include savings, investments, real estate and other possessions of material value. A teenager might have no personal assets currently, but in some states he or she can be held financially liable for some years. Thus, his or her future earnings and assets may be subject to the judgment.

Check the newspaper for information on substantial civil suits which are being brought — and won — against drunk drivers (including teenagers). Note on the chart below how few beers it would take to put your teenage driver on the road drunk or dangerously impaired. Then share this information with your teenage son or daughter.

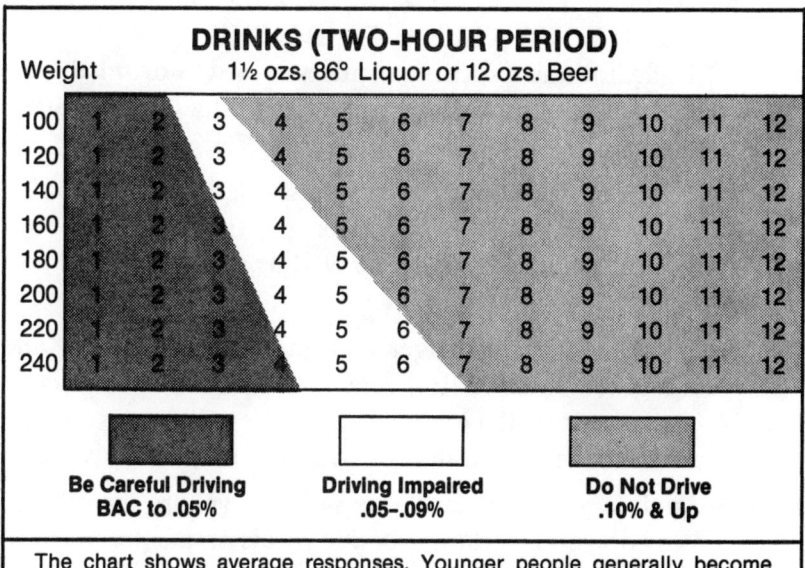

Weight	DRINKS (TWO-HOUR PERIOD) 1½ ozs. 86° Liquor or 12 ozs. Beer										
100	1	2	3	4	5	6	7	8	9	10	11	12
120	1	2	3	4	5	6	7	8	9	10	11	12
140	1	2	3	4	5	6	7	8	9	10	11	12
160	1	2	3	4	5	6	7	8	9	10	11	12
180	1	2	3	4	5	6	7	8	9	10	11	12
200	1	2	3	4	5	6	7	8	9	10	11	12
220	1	2	3	4	5	6	7	8	9	10	11	12
240	1	2	3	4	5	6	7	8	9	10	11	12

Be Careful Driving BAC to .05%
Driving Impaired .05–.09%
Do Not Drive .10% & Up

The chart shows average responses. Younger people generally become impaired sooner, while older people have more vision problems at night. Tests show a wide range of responses even for people of the same age and weight. For some people, one drink may be too many.

What Can Parents Do About Teenage Drinking and Driving Problems?

Anytime your teenager hits the road, he or she is vulnerable to the irrational negligence of drinking drivers. It is estimated that on a weekend night, one out of every ten drivers has been drinking. If your teenager is also drinking, this compounds the risk. What are parents' responsibilities to their teenage driver?

- ✔ The teenage driver must continue not only to sharpen defensive driving skills, but also to heed reasonable precautions which help avoid or minimize the incessant risk of drinking drivers. You can assist your son or daughter in this by setting a good example and sharing your experience.

  - DON'T EVER DRINK AND DRIVE YOURSELF! Your positive example is the single most important thing you can offer to discourage your teenager from drinking and driving. If you come in from a party and Dad smells like scotch, make sure Junior knows Mom drove — and did not drink. Or vice-versa.

- *ALWAYS* FASTEN YOUR SEAT BELT AND INSIST THAT YOUR TEENAGER DO LIKEWISE. Many of the deaths and crippling injuries caused by drunk drivers could have been avoided if the victims had been wearing seat belts.
- Refamiliarize yourself with your state's driver's manual so that you can accurately answer questions and point out the infractions of others, as well as provide a good role model.
- Encourage your teenager's criticism of your driving and accept it without being defensive. Chances are the criticism is justified! This encourages the teenager to criticize a friend's driving if necessary, which may save his life!
- Analyze your own intuitive skills and share them. (e.g., Why do you feel the car beside you is preparing to cut in front of you? What alerts you to expect a car to run the red light at an intersection?)
- Point out to your teenage driver the dangerous areas of the community. What intersections have the most accidents? What traffic lights do motorists tend to run regularly?
- ✔ Impress upon your teenager the tremendous brute force and accompanying responsibility that is assumed when one takes control of a motor vehicle.
- ✔ Make certain that the teenager understands and respects the consequences of drunk and drugged driving practices. Put "loss of license" into a teenager's perspective: You walk; You hitch rides with parents or friends; You don't go. This often has more impact than the threat of a $100 fine.
- ✔ Set up your own point system regarding rules for irresponsible use of the car. Firmly enforce it. Don't hesitate to limit or cancel driving privileges.
- ✔ Insist that your teenager take some responsibility for the car so he or she develops a protective interest in it: helping with auto insurance, paying for gasoline, washing and cleaning the inside regularly, etc.
- ✔ If your teenager ends up in court for a driving offense, be there to support him or her, but don't get the ticket fixed or pay for it yourself.

- ✓ Encourage your teenager to ride only with responsible drivers. Urge your child to call you *any* time of the day or night if he or she needs a safe ride home. Don't limit this appeal to the older teenagers. What if your 12 year old daughter is baby-sitting for a parent who is too impaired to drive her home safely?

- ✓ **UNDER ANY CIRCUMSTANCES** do not tolerate your teenager drinking and driving! Encourage him or her not to tolerate it in others.

- ✓ Prompt all teenagers to assume personal responsibility for keeping drunk drivers off the road. Teach them to recognize the driving pattern of an intoxicated driver. Provide them with the telephone number for reporting an erratic driver. Find out if your state has a REDDI (Report Every Drunk Driver Immediately) program. This could save a life — maybe even yours!

- ✓ Your teenager may be a skillful and conscientious driver, yet still be involved in an accident due to mechanical failure, weather conditions or the negligence of another driver. Make sure he or she knows exactly what to do in case of an accident. This includes knowing how to administer emergency first aid and having the necessary supplies available in the car at all times.

What Are Teenagers Doing About The Problem?

Many teenagers around the country, who care about themselves *and* their friends, are active in various student-directed efforts to combat teen drinking and driving. Perhaps the most prominent organization of this type is SADD (**S**tudents **A**gainst **D**riving **D**runk) which has chapters in communities throughout the nation. SADD takes advantage of peer pressure by promoting a positive image of young people who do not combine drinking and driving.

A very important part of the SADD program involves a reciprocal "Contract for Life" entered into mutually by parent(s) and student. This is an agreement between parents and their teenage sons and daughters to call upon each other to provide safe and sober transportation home any time the need arises. No questions asked — until later. Among other things, this contract opens up a line of communication between parent and teen on a subject that is too often avoided. The reciprocity of it is an admission that drinking and driving is also an adult problem, which often breaks down a teenager's defensive attitude. A new SADD "Contract For Life — Between Friends" is also available for students who, for some reason, feel unable to ask their parents for this kind of back up.

However, joint signatures on this contract don't automatically insure your teenage drinker's safety on the road. The parent advisor of a SADD chapter in Colorado says, "I wish the two D's in SADD stood for drinking and driving, rather than driving drunk. We have seen too many kids thinking it's okay to drink and drive, as long as they don't drive drunk. They then decide themselves at what point they (or the drinking drivers they are with) are 'too drunk' to drive. By that time, their judgment is already impaired by alcohol. The SADD program really says don't drink — at all — and drive. A 'designated driver' is the only answer for anyone who drinks and then needs to get somewhere."

Some students who like to "party" alternately designate one of their group as the non-drinking driver, responsible for getting them all home safely. Yet, this designated driver approach is not fail-safe either unless common sense is used. For example, if there is drinking "before" or "on the way," the non-drinking designated driver must be responsible for getting friends "there" as well as home. Some party givers require that everyone turn in their car keys when they arrive at a party. They are returned only if the driver passes a sobriety test. However, at large, chaotic parties such as those described in the previous section, this well-intentioned effort too, can fall apart, if not well organized. While these practices and others like them certainly don't eliminate the dangers of teen drinking parties, they can help decrease the teenage drunk driving statistics. And until we reverse the teen social drinking trend, that's the name of the game.

4. Practical Prevention

THE CASE AGAINST TEENAGE DRINKING

A teenager usually will not challenge a conscientious parent about the propriety of using drugs such as marijuana and cocaine. Possession or use of such substances is clearly illegal and heavily penalized — even for adults. Use of alcohol seems to be another matter. Drinking age laws insult a teenager's idealistic sense of fair play. Your teen may eventually confront you with the question, "What's the big deal about my drinking? You drink!"

Under normal circumstances, parents who are responsible drinkers are not expected to abstain while their kids are teenagers. However, they should be very conscious of the example they are setting. They also should be well-armed to answer their teenager's recriminating questions rationally. "Adults are different — period" is not an acceptable answer to adolescents. Nor will they accept "It's illegal — period!" Why is there legislation in every state regarding drinking age? What's wrong with kids drinking?

Avoid copping out of these questions with glib, defensive answers like "Drinking teens all become alcoholics and get into serious trouble with the police" or "Teens who drink are sick-looking wimps." Eventually, as your child becomes exposed to healthy looking teenage friends who are both popular and successful at athletics, — and who drink — he or she will discover your explanation is not necessarily true. You will have lost your credibility, and your teenager may become much more inclined to experiment.

The fact is that the teenage body is in a critical stage of physical, mental and emotional development, which can be curtailed by early alcohol use or abuse. The ability to make reasonable judgments can be impaired at a time when lifelong patterns are being established. Another factor to consider is noted by Robert L.

DuPont, M.D., who says, "The earlier a young person uses alcohol, the more likely he or she is to use it excessively with adverse consequences, and the more likely that young person is to add other drugs to alcohol, starting with marijuana and progressing to cocaine and other drugs." Why not give your child fact rather than fiction? Consider modifying some of the following suggestions for your own particular needs.

The Physical Aspect

Refamiliarize yourself with the section of this booklet which addresses alcohol and its effects. Your teenager, undoubtedly, has been exposed to these facts in school drug education programs, but has he ever considered them in relation to his own lifestyle? How they might apply to him and his friends? Has he considered, for example, that the health problems associated with heavy alcohol use take time to surface, that the good football player on the high school team might become a Heisman Trophy winner instead of just a good player were he not abusing his body with alcohol?

Does he know that the teenage body, not yet fully developed, may often react to alcohol erratically? Thus a teenager is prone to become intoxicated more quickly and to a greater degree than a comparable-sized adult. Many experts say a teenager is more susceptible to alcohol addiction. A teenager who elects to use alcohol, therefore, may be assuming a greater risk than he is prepared to handle.

The Mental Aspect

Obviously, if a teenager's brain is sluggish due to alcohol consumed the previous afternoon, evening or even the previous weekend, he may have trouble concentrating on the material presented in his classes. Ideally, formal education sharpens the student's ability to take available facts, analyze them, and arrive at a logical conclusion or course of action. If the student's use of alcohol prevents him from learning the pertinent facts *and* prevents or drastically delays the formation of mental processing skills, the years in school do little to prepare the student for the future. In later years, a high school graduate may find himself without the *ability* necessary to accomplish what he wants in later life. He may be unprepared or lag far behind his peers in college, trade school, on-the-job training, etc. Alcohol use can also interfere with motivation. What are your teen's plans for the future? Can premature use of alcohol interfere with these plans?

The Emotional Aspect

In addition to digesting and interpreting a multitude of known facts, the teenage mind is going through a critical process of emotional development between the ages of 12 and 18. At this age, children are establishing lifelong patterns of coping emotionally with whatever life deals out. How a teenager deals with an unreasonable teacher at 15 will probably influence how he or she handles an unreasonable boss at 35. Habitual or semi-habitual use of alcohol at this age is apt to retard this maturation process. According to Dr. Jorge Valles, former Director of Alcoholism Therapy at the U.S. Veterans Hospital in Houston, Texas, the hypothalamus section of the brain does not fully develop and mature until somewhere between the ages of 20 and 22. "The action of the alcohol is channeled directly toward the adolescent's imbalanced hypothalamus and autonomic nervous system, thereby obstructing his emotional maturation on both psychological and physiological levels," says Dr. Valles.* Thus, the necessary adolescent experiences of learning to cope may be arrested by early alcohol use. Whether this essential period of development can ever be fully regained is not known. A teenager who habitually uses alcohol to escape from stressful situations or to give him a false courage may eventually grow into a 35-year-old who has the emotional maturity and coping skills of a pre-teen.

Learning to cope is not limited to the more structured and serious times in an adolescent's life. Handling social encounters is also vital in discovering how to cope effectively, particularly with the issues of identity and peer relationships E including those with the opposite sex. Many teenagers drink in the numerous teen social settings where alcohol is available because they are tense, anxious, worried or nervous about the social experience. Alcohol not only relaxes them, but it also takes away their incentive to engage in productive social interaction — one of the most important parts of the adolescent experience.

---

* The commentary by Dr. Jorge Valles appears in a brochure entitled "What Parents Must Learn About Teens and Alcohol" by Mary Jo Green, Parent Coordinator of the National Federation of Parents for Drug-Free Youth.

The Judgment Aspect

Alcohol can dangerously impair the judgment of adults as well as teenagers. However, since judgment is the result of life experience, teenagers who have lived fewer years in a relatively protected environment, naturally, do not have as solid a base for good judgment as does an adult. Therefore, *any* impairment of their still limited judgmental skills can lead to disastrous consequences. A case in point is the inexperienced teenage driver who drinks two beers and then drives. Review with your teenager the level by level effect of alcohol on the brain. Point out how the mind's ability to integrate information and make sound judgments deteriorates when affected by alcohol.

A Note For Parents

Parents should keep in mind that in a few short years, today's teens will be young adults who can legally choose to drink or not to drink. For that reason, it is recommended that parents make certain their teenagers are explicitly aware of the potential negative effects of various chemical substances — particularly alcohol — and the risks associated with their use. These risks include the legal liabilities resulting from irresponsible alcohol use.

If your teenager delays the decision to use alcohol until he or she is of legal drinking age, the young adult is more likely to decide against such use. However, if the young person does decide *at that time* to start alcohol use, he or she is considered less likely to progress to heavy, out-of-control use or to add other drugs to the mix than if use had begun at an earlier age.

WHAT YOU CAN DO WITHIN YOUR OWN FAMILY

The most effective solution to the adolescent drug epidemic is prevention! Start now and think through what your attitudes and policies are going to be about teenage drinking and other drug use. Realize that those policies may be subject to change to accommodate a changing family situation. Parents should try to reach agreement with each other about the ways they will handle the drug issue in their family. There should be consistency and mutual support in communicating with your child.

An Informed Parent Is A Child's Best Weapon

Become informed on every aspect of the problem as it might affect your child growing up in your community. Know about specific drugs and their effects. Be aware of the current drug scene, particularly the teen scene. In addition to the information you find in this booklet, information is available at the local public and school libraries, as well as the sources listed in Appendix K. Talk to other parents, teachers, youth counselors, police officers and neighbors. The more you know, the more credible you are when talking to your teenagers about the alcohol/drug issue.

Tactfully initiate discussions about various aspects of the local teenage alcohol/drug scene, making it a shared interest. Reinforce what your teenagers have learned in school and continue their education about legal and illegal drugs. Put it into perspective for them. When you hear or read about tragedies or near tragedies involving teenagers, alcohol and other drugs, discuss those tragedies.

Observe your teenager; spend time with him and listen to his feelings. Be alert for signs of use, but don't act overly suspicious. The latter could appear to be mistrust, which might block open communication.

Confront The Issue Before There Is A Problem

- ✔ Make clear your own case against teenage alcohol and other drug use. If you object to such use for personal reasons such as alcoholism or addiction in the family, religious beliefs, susceptibility to diabetes or hypoglycemia, etc., be honest about those reasons. Generally, it is best not to make the drug issue a moral one.

- ✔ Explain that the changes, conflicts, and mood swings are normal. Emphasize that learning to deal with depression, pressure, etc., without chemical aid is a necessary part of becoming an adult.

- ✔ When you state you will not allow your teenager to use drugs, you assume you can exert total control over his or her life — which is impossible. So don't leave it at that. Sit down with your teenager, discuss your expectations and ask for input. Adolescents will respond better if they feel they've been heard. They also respect a parent who isn't afraid to take a firm stance.

- ✔ Set limits. Focus on the most critical potential problems and strive for a reasonable balance between control and autonomy. Healthy ground rules encourage individual and family growth potential, and foster open, honest communication. Rules must be flexible enough that they can be readjusted and/or restructured when the situation warrants it. However, they must not change spasmodically or according to whom they are being applied. Be consistent! Don't feel obligated to conform to other parents' rules.

- ✔ Be willing to enforce your limits. Adolescents *need* parental guidance! They want parents to be parents! Don't be fooled by their exterior; often they appear to be rejecting you when really they are testing the boundaries you have set as well as your commitment to them. Establish fair but effective punishments.

- ✔ Emphasize that you trust your teenager, but that you don't trust his or her inexperience. Also let the teenager know that trust must be earned. Be careful not to *burden* him or her with too much trust. Parents can set their youngsters up for failure by allowing them to get into a position they are emotionally unprepared to handle or shouldn't be asked to handle, for example, by allowing a dozen 15-year-old boys *and* girls to go to a mountain condo for an unchaperoned ski weekend. Similarly, parents should think twice about leaving a 14-year-old in charge of the unchaperoned house and younger siblings, while they take a week's vacation.

Let Teenagers Know That You Are Concerned Because You Care

Too often, adolescents misinterpret their parents' motives in exerting authority. They feel their parents are merely trying to spoil their good time. Parents may falsely give the impression they are extracting payment for a debt which the teenagers feel they don't owe (the "after all I've done for you" syndrome). Teenagers can feel that a parent is jealous of their peer relationships and freedom from serious responsibility — particularly if the parent is beset with problems. It is important to go out of your way to let them know how much you care, so they will understand why you are concerned about where they are and what they are doing.

- ✔ Be *for* your kids and let them know it! You may not always agree with their actions, but you can still be excited about your children as people. A big hug from time to time can say a lot.

- ✔ Recognize and encourage their natural talents and extra curricular activities. Success develops healthy self-esteem which, in turn, deters drug use. Positive activities leave your children less time to get in trouble.

- ✔ Don't concentrate solely on rooting out bad behavior and punishing it. Take pains to notice good traits and compliment them. Reward good behavior with special privileges.

- ✔ Be available for your kids. During adolescence a lot of "crises" will occur that cannot be scheduled. Your availability at such a time will speak volumes about your commitment to them.

- ✔ Think through ways that you can become meaningfully involved in *their* lives. This might include spending time with them in sports, shopping, concerts, school or outside activities, etc.

Help Your Child Develop Decision-Making Skills

Mom and Dad may say to their teenager, "Well, now that you're growing up, make your own decision." Yet, they may have never taught the child basic decision-making skills. Faced with an alcohol and drug oriented teen society, parents' ultimate goal should be enabling their child to say "no." One reason adolescents use alcohol and other drugs is because they can't cope with stress caused by the problems in their lives. Perhaps, they have never learned any practical problem-solving techniques. Decision-making is a tool for problem-solving. Parents have the responsibility to help their teenager develop these skills.

You should begin to teach your child at an early age to go through a logical decision-making process. Start with simple decisions of no major consequence and work up to the more complicated and important ones. For example, a young child might periodically be given the responsibility to decide what TV program the entire family should watch. Then, as he gets older, let him determine, for example, whether to use his savings earmarked for a car now or wait until he graduates. Does he need a car at all? The child must also learn very early to accept the consequences of his or her decisions. For example, if siblings revolt at her choice of a TV program, she must handle the conflict. If the repairs on his second-hand car are $100 a month, it's his problem.

Seek active involvement in the earlier stages of the learning process. Then gradually, as the adolescent becomes more proficient, assign more responsibility for decision-making and withdraw your participation to an appropriate point. The process of "letting go" is discussed in more depth later in this section.

It's unlikely you will be present when your teenager is offered drugs or urged to do something else illegal and/or dangerous, such as riding home with a drunk driver. However, let your teenager know you are always available as a sounding-board. Likewise, if you sense a serious problem which the child seems reluctant to discuss, subtly encourage him or her to share it with you. Your teenager must recognize, though, that as long as he or she is financially dependent on you, and you are legally liable for his or her actions, you have the right to exercise final authority at any time. In other words, you have the responsibility and the parental right to make *any* non-abusive decision regarding your dependent child, when, in your own mind, the seriousness of the situation warrants it. Surprisingly, the child's reaction to this may be relief rather than resentment. When this course of action is required, let your example serve to reinforce the principles of good decision-making.

What are these principles and how are they used? Let's go to the bottom line.

- ✔ Define the problem. Example: John wants me to try crack with him.

- ✔ Identify the alternatives. Example: Yes or no.

- ✔ Weigh the pros and cons of each alternative. Example:

    Pro — I'd like to see what it feels like. It's a short high, so I wouldn't risk going home blasted. I have the ten bucks.

    Con — I saw on TV that crack is really addictive. Those two athletes just dropped dead from cocaine. If I use my ten bucks for crack, I can't buy the new Alabama tape.

    Urge your child to consider the worst possible consequence of each alternative. Example: Pro — I could drop dead from one hit of crack. Not good! Con — I may never know what it feels like to smoke crack. So what? I may never know about cyanide either.

✔ Make the decision and go for it. Example: "Naw. I don't have ten bucks for that. See ya' around."

Help Build Your Child's Self-Confidence and Self-Esteem

Two very important factors which contribute to positive self-image are self-confidence and self-esteem. These positive states of mind must be nurtured carefully to produce self-confident and capable young people who feel good about themselves — young people who are much more inclined to say "no" to alcohol and other drugs. The cultivating of a child's self-image is an important part of preventive parenting.

Adolescents, by nature, are often painfully cruel, somewhat fickle and grossly inconsiderate of each others' feelings. Even "best friends" sometimes tear each other down in a selfish effort to feel good about themselves. Occasionally, an insensitive teacher or a coach obsessed with winning will contribute to a child's feelings of inadequacy. Consequently, a child may be in trouble if he or she must depend solely on peers and disinterested adult authority for the development of self-image.

There are many subtle ways of helping a child develop self-confidence and self-esteem. References to several of them are scattered throughout this book. However, most of them fall into two main categories: (1). Praise. (2). Helping children realize their own unique abilities and limitations. The following comments may help you develop your own style of self-image building.

Praise

- Kids may resent parents who praise only what the parent considers to be major accomplishments: A dad who only applauds a winning touchdown or a mom who only gets excited about making the honor roll. "Yeah, they liked that. But nothing else I do is right." Don't overlook or take for granted the more minor day-to-day accomplishments which may be much more meaningful to the child personally than academic or athletic achievement.

- Praise teenagers at every opportunity, but the praise must be deserved to be meaningful and constructive. On a bad day you may have to resort to commenting on the beautiful color of their eyes (or hair or teeth). The important thing is to consistently make teenagers feel good about some aspect of themselves.

- Recognize your teenager's effort! What is spectacular for one adolescent may not be spectacular for another. A teenager should always be praised effusively for doing the very best job he or she is capable of under the existing circumstances. A peer may do the job better, but the peer may have more natural talent for the task and have to put forth very little effort.

Unique Abilities

- Your teenager may not possess the particular natural talents you would prefer. Accept this and help the young person discover the talents he or she does have. Help them to appreciate fully their unique capabilities by showing your own appreciation. Launch a concentrated effort to encourage the development of these capabilities.

- Actively support the child's efforts. Attend the athletic event, art exhibit or science fair. Assist in finding a second-hand guitar. Actions do speak louder than words.

- Don't just *tell* teenagers to do a task. *Show* them how to do it right. Work with them until they become reasonably proficient. Each skill mastered will strengthen the foundation needed to build overall self-confidence.

Unique Limitations

- When appropriate let your teenager know you recognize and accept his or her limitations. At the same time, indicate how much you appreciate his capabilities. Example: "Yes, you are too slightly built to go out for football. But your graceful build is why the girls say you're the "coolest" looking dancer around. More importantly, encourage teenagers to accept their limitations and learn to compensate with their abilities. Avoid making this a "put-down" confrontation. You might share a personal disappointment from your own youth and explain how you handled it.

- Occasionally a teenager is determined to pursue a goal which, it seems, he (or she) can't possibly accomplish. That's a tough situation to deal with. He might surprise you. On the other hand, he may withdraw into deeper depression with each successive failure. Probably you admire his stick-to-itiveness and thus may feel you owe him your support. However, that doesn't mean you can't still try to distract him with other activities, and tactfully encourage frequent repetitions of the decision-making process.

Nurture The Family As A Supportive Refuge For The Adolescent

Family life in America today is under both internal and external pressures. Yet, despite the strain, it still can be one of the most effective sources of strength and positive influence for an adolescent confronted with the teenage alcohol/drug scene.

- Even though adolescents are normally "breaking away," they need a positive relationship which makes them feel a part of something greater than self, such as family, country, a God, etc.

- Children need identification with successful role models whom they respect. Such models are often found somewhere within the family group. A strong sense of "family" usually engenders mutual pride and respect which makes the positive family role model a potentially effective prevention tool.

- Caring parents can build a child's inner defenses against alcohol/drug use: feelings of self-worth, the ability to defer gratification and exert self-discipline, the self-confidence to say "no," etc.

- Children need to feel they are responsible and useful members of their family. Ask your teenager to list all obligations (homework, cleaning his or her room, yardwork, etc.) and then let the teenager decide and commit to exactly how and when they will be met.

Be Aware Of Who Your Teenagers Role Models Are

Parents' attitudes and behavior have a strong effect on their children. Be aware that your own use of legal drugs (prescription, non-prescription and alcohol) serves as a powerful role model for your son or daughter. Be responsible! Adolescents are amazingly adept at figuring out what their parents are up to. Mom and Dad are making a naive assumption if they think their teenager is unaware of parental drug abuse or illegal and irresponsible use of drugs. Whether parents realize it or not, this type of parental behavior transmits a loud and clear "do-drug" message and/or promotes the idea that "laws are made to be broken."

Role models other than parents might include parents' friends, relatives, teachers, coaches, or celebrities, older brothers and sisters, people for whom they babysit, etc. What impression could abuse or irresponsible use of alcohol and other drugs by these role models make on your teenager? Are the celebrities your teenager admires (rock stars, sports figures, etc.) negative role models who transmit "do-drug" messages via rock music, beer commercials or their private lives? It might be wise to find out.

Recognize And Pattern Social Needs Early

Kids want to be together. Doing something is secondary. Parents can help plan activities (even just having a few friends over to watch TV) and arrange transportation. If there are not planned and supervised activities, the young teenagers who are without wheels will start to "hang out" and that's where the trouble begins. Helping them plan interesting activities when they're in the early teens is a safeguard against teenagers moving into the upper grades with the idea that a beer party is the only worthwhile game in town.

Help Your Teenager Set Challenging Goals

Without long-range goals, a teenager is subject to short-term frustration, which in some cases can lead to drug use. In addition, nothing raises self-esteem more than measurable success in attaining goals.

✔ Motivate your teenager to set realistic long-term goals for himself (or herself) and to reevaluate them periodically.

These might include: summer plans, developing a particular talent, scholastic achievement, saving for a graduation trip, college plans, career goals, etc.

✔ Encourage him to also set intermediate, easily attainable goals. A major goal broken into several smaller tasks, or sub-goals, makes the overall project seem less awesome and provides an opportunity for success in several areas.

✔ Provide the inspiration necessary for him to believe in his ability to change the course of his life through his own actions.

Assist Your Teenager In Setting Down A Value System

Values are important for an adolescent — even though he or she may be unwilling to admit it. Emerging adults should recognize the need for sorting out personal values conscientiously. If they don't know their own values, it's difficult for them to effectively weigh pros and cons during the decision-making process. Problem-solving may then become simply a matter of the "wants" and the "don't wants." Thus, youngsters with scattered values are often more susceptible to drug use.

- Encourage your teenager to analyze more abstractly and make moral decisions of wrong versus right.

- Casually and without bias, ask your teenager how he or she feels about controversial issues, people, situations, etc. Challenge teenagers to think seriously about what their values are.

Perhaps religion should also be addressed in the context of value systems. In his excellent book entitled *Getting Tough on Gateway Drugs*, Robert L. DuPont, Jr., M. D. emphasizes the role of religion in the prevention and treatment of drug dependence. He states, "In the context of drug abuse prevention, religion is a way to escape the limitations of the biologically based pleasure system for controlling behavior by seeing beyond individualistic, present-tense pleasure to larger human values and purposes. As such, religion is, at the least, a helpful part of drug abuse prevention and, at most, an indispensable part of real recovery." Dr. DuPont's assessment of the positive preventive role of religion is confirmed by other experts.

Communicate

In order for parents to guide and support a young person through the difficult teenage years, they must understand what their child is feeling, thinking, saying and doing. How often do parents wonder why they can communicate so much better with their children's friends than with their own teenager? In part, it may be because parents have no vested interest in their teenager's friends. Therefore, they are free to communicate on a courteous, uninvolved, social level.

Likewise, during this booklet's preparation, many adolescents complained to us resentfully that they were unable to talk to their parents because the parents couldn't understand or wouldn't listen. The bottom line may be that parents need to review some principles of effective communication.

- ✔ Be an "askable" parent. Create opportunities to discuss "nothing in particular."

    - Casual one-on-one communication is important because it encourages confidences. Periodically Mom or Dad might take their teenager for a Saturday lunch, an "after-homework" ice cream, etc. Doing chores together such as cleaning house or yard work can also be a time for just "shooting the breeze."

    - Assign high priority to the daily "sit-down" family meal, even though it's difficult for a very active family to manage. Make meals a special time for sharing among family members.

- ✔ By example stimulate your teenager to listen, communicate feelings, and relate to others.

- ✔ When you must set an additional limit, do it in a manner calculated to minimize resentment and save self-esteem. Convey authority, not insult.

- ✔ If possible, when you have a specific issue to discuss with your teenager, set a convenient time and place that is private and free of distractions and interruptions. Don't consistently trap him or her in the car on the way to school.

    - Gather your facts beforehand and organize them logically. Be receptive to new data. Plan carefully in your mind how you will use the facts to present your case.

- Understand your own motivation in regard to the issue.
- Remember that conflict is a problem situation arising out of different opinions, needs, goals, etc. Conflict may be settled by:

  Argument — if there is a single correct solution.

  Compromise — if there are multiple correct solutions.

✓ When your child wants to talk with you about something important, do it immediately or as soon as possible. Later, a teenager may have changed his mind about discussing it.

- Don't dismiss the impact of an adolescent crisis because it seems trivial by adult standards.
- Reinforce your youngster's desire to talk with you: for example, "Thanks for sharing this with me."
- Listen carefully and with obvious interest to what your child is telling you. Don't continually interrupt to make a point.
- Let your children know you respect and empathize with their feelings even though you may not agree with them.
- Get all the facts. Open-ended questions elicit more self-exploration and discussion of the topic.
- When appropriate, restate the facts and the feelings, to ascertain that you understand. Don't automatically jump to conclusions.
- Ask your teenager how he or she wants you to help: Advice on identifying the available options? Helping weigh the pros and cons of the various options? Taking an appropriate action?

✓ Be aware of your facial expressions, eye contact and body language. Without uttering one word, narrowed eyes or a clenched fist can abruptly terminate a positive conversational mood and put your teenager on the defensive.

✓ Be careful how you phrase things.

- Use the first person when possible: "I have a problem with your . . ."
- Avoid accusatory statements.

WHAT YOU CAN DO IN YOUR "NEIGHBORHOOD"

As your children get older, both your concept of "neighborhood" and theirs is constantly enlarged and rearranged. At any one time it may include several actual neighborhoods within the school attendance area. In a larger city the 6th grade classes of 75-100 students merge and become one middle and high school class of 500 or more students representing many geographical neighborhood areas. Your mission is to integrate all of these new people and places into your own sense of "neighborhood." This is often a difficult task which requires persistence and assertive effort.

Know Your Teenager's Friends

Teenagers' friends are important to them *and* to you. Friends constitute a peer support group as your children gradually break close parental ties. This group can have far-reaching positive or negative influence. It is critical for you to establish positive relationships with these young people.

- Know who your teenager's friends are. Listen for names. Show genuine interest when your child discusses them. Encourage your teenager to invite friends into your home. A fringe benefit of making your home a place for the peer group to gather is that it enables you to subtly supervise and possibly counter their "hangin' out" with positive activities.

- Take time to visit with your teenager's friends. Let them know that you recognize them as people in their own right. Show an interest in their opinions and activities. Make them feel welcome in your home!

- Be a parent and resist the temptation to become one of them. Maintain an open door policy that encourages a special positive relationship between parent and teen. Be as fair and empathetic to your teenager's friends as you are to your own teen, but let them know what your behavioral expectations are.

- Listen to them. Their problem may also be *your* teenager's problem. Solicited advice you give your child's friend may be passed on by that friend to your own son or daughter at a later date.

- Consider their respect important! The more openness *and* mutual respect there is in your relationship with your teenager and his or her friends, the better your opportunity to effectively confront them with issues of concern — such as teenage drinking, the party scene, etc.

- Encourage them to trust you. Don't forget, trust is earned. If you make a promise, keep it! Should a crisis occur where a parent's involvement is crucial, THEY WILL CALL YOU IF THEY TRUST YOU!

Choosing their own friends and building new social relationships is essential for good adjustment in later life. But, occasionally a teenager picks a friend who is undesirable for one reason or another — perhaps the friend uses drugs. Avoid openly criticizing such a friend, as teenagers are extremely loyal to one another. If you forbid your children to associate with someone, be prepared to keep track of or supervise their every waking moment.

Another alternative is to unobtrusively distract your teenager with an irresistible activity which, by its nature, must exclude the undesirable friend. Perhaps a casual discussion of good friends in general — which naturally flows into a discussion of that friend in particular — may motivate the child to consider the pros and cons of the relationship. Teenagers usually pick friends who complement the attitudes and values they already have. Perhaps you need to examine your own child's values.

Know The Parents Of Your Teenager's Friends

Establish an open line of communication with the parents of your teenager's peer group *before* a crisis develops. It doesn't matter how you do it — just do it. If you wait to casually run into them at Back-To-School Night or a ball game, you may wait forever. You might call the parents, introduce yourself as ____'s Mom or Dad and let them know that you want to touch base. If you are so inclined, have your youngster's friends *and* their parents over for an informal get-together, perhaps a potluck meal or a dessert party.

Why is this so important?

- It gives you an opportunity to size them up. Are they approachable/ distant, involved/disinterested, strict/permissive, open-minded/ defensive, reasonable/irrational? Do they appear to be in control of their teenager? Does there seem to be a good relationship between parent and child? Are they the kind of people who will keep something in strict confidence, such as information that your teenager has told you about their son's or daughter's activities?

- It gives *them* an opportunity to size you up for the same reasons. Over the middle school and high school years, there may be things about your child you will never be told if no one knows you, or if you have a reputation of being a defensive or disinterested parent.

  - Not only is a peer parent "grapevine" (network) invaluable in keeping up with what the kids are *really* doing, but also the kids become sensitive to the fact that an effective "grapevine" is in operation. They know they have to plan "trouble" very carefully, and often it just isn't worth it.

  - When parents of a peer group communicate, they can present a united front as far as curfews, allowable activities, etc. This makes it easier on kids and parents because it dilutes social pressure for undesirable activities and hours.

Don't let yourself become a victim of parental peer pressure when you feel that you are in the right! Likewise, don't hesitate to let your teenager know you feel another parent is just plain wrong and why. If you go along with something that is against your established principles because you are afraid to openly condemn it, your teenager may think you are hypocritical when you urge *him or her* not to yield to peer pressure.

Create A Parent Network In Your Neighborhood

Call the parents of several of your teenager's neighborhood friends and tell them of your concerns. Invite them to a meeting (set time and place). Ask each of them to call several people they know. At the meeting, express your own personal concerns and ask each one, in turn, to express theirs. Just listen. Then ask them to brainstorm for a list of issues to be discussed at length.

> Suggestions: curfews, responsibility, how you handle money, house rules, friends, acceptable modes of behavior, personal experiences with alcohol, drugs and your kids, etc.

You will probably find you only begin to get started discussing these issues on the first meeting. Plan to meet periodically, and appoint someone to organize calling for reminders. If other parents start to show an interest, include them, whether they live in your neighborhood or not. Or help them start a network in their own neighborhood.

WHAT YOU CAN DO WITHIN YOUR OWN COMMUNITY

The normal adolescent hang-ups, the availability and effects of alcohol and other drugs, the teen environment outside the home, and the community as a whole, all interact to affect your teenager's attitude toward and involvement in the alcohol/drug scene. Anything relating to these four factors directly or indirectly affects *your* teenager. Your awareness and involvement impresses upon your teen how serious you are about your position on these issues.

Be Aware Of School And Community Issues And Activities

- Be informed about legislative activity pertaining to drugs, drunk driving, etc. Be aware of school district policies regarding substance abuse. To gauge the climate of the community and keep informed about the issues, carefully read the parent/teacher group newsletter, the student newspaper, the school district news, and the school student handbook — in addition to your local community newspaper.

- Attend as many parent meetings and activities as possible, both at school and in your neighborhood. They are an excellent source of information — and not just about the topic officially under discussion. An amazing number of informational gems about the teen "party" scene, problems at the school, etc. surface at such meetings.

- Find out what positive activities are available for teenagers in your community. Recreational activities, organized sports, and classes on hobbies or other interesting subjects may be available through the school, a parks and recreation department, a community center, the YMCA/YWCA or other groups. In some areas community colleges offer helpful classes for teenagers. These might include stress management classes, assertiveness training, and communication workshops.

- Get your name on selected mailing lists: your local alcohol and drug task force, The National Federation of Parents for Drug-Free Youth, PRIDE, MADD, SADD, etc.

Get Involved! Your Involvement Can Effect Positive Change

- Support teenagers in their efforts to create a social world that does not revolve around alcohol and other drugs. Get as involved in helping with student activities as your time permits. Call the school activities director and offer to chaperone a dance or field trip. Work with other athletic team or club parents to plan a social event after a game/club meeting. Become actively involved in parent/teacher group activities, task force groups, etc.

- If there is no task force on youth and drugs in your community, start one. A group of parents in action is a positive and powerful tool to use in combatting the teenage alcohol and drug problem in a community. Put a notice in your local newspaper describing the concept and setting an organizational meeting date. Or just telephone a few people. If you can interest just one other person, you're on your way. Thousands of communities have formed task force groups in the past five years, often at the determined instigation of one person. Contact the National Federation of Parents for Alcohol-Drug Free Youth, PRIDE, or the NIDA Hotline for information. The addresses and toll-free numbers are in Appendix K, along with the names of several books which address the subject of parent groups in action.

- Be willing to bring an overlooked drug/alcohol issue to public attention. Contact the president of your parent/teacher organization, a task force board member, a city council member, a legislator, the police department, the local newspaper, etc.

- Some of the prevention effort must be aimed at decreasing both the supply of and the demand for addictive drugs. Offer to assist with petitions regarding pertinent issues if you feel strongly about them. Attend public hearings on businesses affecting the community's teen population.

- Get involved *with your teenager* in a community project to help others. Youngsters need an opportunity not only to feel a part of the community as a whole, but also to give of themselves outside their school experience.

NOTES FOR SINGLE PARENTS

A person who was an effective parent before a divorce will, most likely, be an effective parent after a divorce. Successful single parents indicate, though, that there are new factors that need to be plugged into the parenting formula following a divorce. Consider a few:

- ✔ Divorce, if not thoughtfully handled by parents, can intensify the fear, anxiety, guilt and questions regarding self that are already a problem for most normal adolescents. How it is expressed is unique to the individual child, but it could include the use of alcohol and/or other drugs.

- ✔ Open hostility between divorced parents is traumatic for adolescents. If you put down your "ex" in front of your teenager, you are risking his resenting you, as well as undermining his respect for *his* mom or dad. You may also be undermining your child's respect for himself, as the biological child of that "no-good" parent. Low self-esteem is often a major factor in a teenager's decision to use drugs.

- ✔ When parents, married or divorced, are divided on an issue involving behavioral expectations (teen drinking, curfews, etc.), children are apt to play mom and dad off against each other to get what they want. This "child-in-control" syndrome is usually intensified by divorce. If the parents are unable to reach an agreement between themselves, they might seriously consider consulting a family or adolescent counselor.

Suggestions From A Divorced Couple

- Both parents need to take care that each is looked upon as a real parent, rather than one a disciplinarian and one a recreation director.

- Both homes need to be fully functioning households with similar house rules. A sensible routine with regular time for meals, recreation, etc. helps assure the youngsters that mom and dad are capable of being on top of any crisis.

Suggestions From a Divorced Parent and a Stepparent

- When the teenager gets in trouble

    A teenager in trouble needs to know that *both* parents are concerned, willing to help, and able to present a united front on his or her behalf — regardless of their personal hang-ups about each other.

    The custodial parent is sometimes hesitant to be completely open with (or even notify) an ex-spouse about a problem, because he or she may feel guilty, expect to be blamed, or fear reprisal, such as a custody suit. If at all possible, be totally open and honest about the details of the problem, even if it is somewhat painful.

    Look at the facts as they stand and go *forward* toward a solution. Resist the temptation to assign blame in retrospect.

    When you come up with a game plan acceptable to both parents, support each other's position one hundred percent.

- Involving stepparents

    Try to put aside for the moment any dislike, resentment, etc. you may feel toward your child's stepparent. He or she is part of your child's family, and regardless of your feelings, *is* involved — directly or indirectly.

    A stepparent who is liked and respected as an adult (minus the stigma an adolescent often attaches to parents) can be an adult friend to your teenager. As such, he or she is able to exert a type of peer influence.

    A willing stepparent, using both parents' input, *may* be able to get to the core of the problem and affect a solution more effectively than either parent.

    If the stepparent does get involved positively, let him or her know in some way that you are appreciative.

Suggestions From A Widowed Mother

- Don't fall into the trap of doing everything for your children because they don't have a dad.
- Help them structure their free time with chores at home, jobs, and activities to be done by the time the parent arrives home.

- Feel confident about decisions you make concerning your child. You know that child better than anyone.

- *Be consistent!* That is probably the hardest thing to do when you are a single parent. You get tired, and it is hard to keep from wearing down. Young adults with dependency problems are wonderful at manipulation.

Approximately 25% of American children are growing up in single parent homes headed by mothers. Single parents, particularly mothers, often feel guilty that they cannot provide their children with the opportunities available in a two-parent home. Joan Herst, a practicing psychotherapist and a columnist for *The Denver Post*, recently answered a question from a divorced mother:

Q. — "Is it true that strong character comes from a dad who is supportive?"

A. — "Absolutely not! It's *easier* to raise children in a home with two supportive parents, but that has nothing to do with character."

Ms. Herst goes on to define character. "...establishing sound ethical values in your youngsters, helping them to see themselves as capable individuals and showing them by example that each person is responsible for his or her own actions. You can accomplish this by living it."

SUGGESTED PARENTING GUIDELINES*

When Your Teenager Is Going Out For The Evening

- Know where he/she is and with whom. Let him/her know where you will be. Advise each other of a change of plans.

- Be aware of transportation arrangements or provide transportation to and from parties, games, etc.

---

*Compiled with the assistance of Mountain Area Families In Action (MAFIA), Evergreen, Colorado.

- Establish the time he/she is expected to return home and expect to be notified if there is a delay.
  Be awake when he/she is due home.

- Make it easy for teenagers to leave a party. Assure them that they can phone you (or a designated adult) to be picked up whenever needed — no questions asked. Urge them to phone you if things get out of hand.

- Call the parent in charge of an activity to verify the occasion, location and duration, adult supervision, policy on alcohol, etc. If the activity seems inappropriate, express your concern and encourage alternative activities.

When Your Teenager Is Having A Few Friends In For The Afternoon Or Evening

- Agree with your teenager on ground rules — time span, number of friends, where in the house they intend to be, no alcohol or drugs.

- Determine how to deal with a friend possessing alcohol or other drugs or under the influence of either. Don't allow anyone under the influence to drive or go home alone. Decide how an uninvited and unwelcome youngster will be handled.

- Pre-arrange a place where the teenagers may "hang out" to talk, watch TV or video tapes, play the stereo, play games, etc. Have snacks and beverages available.

- Ask your teenager to introduce friends you don't know. From that point, be periodically visible and available, but keep a VERY LOW profile for the remainder of the afternoon or evening.

Suggested Hours

- There are curfew laws for teenagers under 18 in many areas of the country, for example, 11 p.m. week nights and 12 a.m. Friday and Saturday. In some areas, tickets are issued to curfew violators *and* their parents. Generally, the child can be taken into custody and held until release to his or her parents. A fine and/or court appearance could also result. To be safe, check out the local laws before setting your teenager's curfew.

PRACTICAL PREVENTION | 91

- Discourage teenagers from going out on school nights except for school activities, community events or adult-sanctioned activities.

- The following are generally accepted weekend hours, except for special events such as proms, homecoming, etc.:

7th grade	10:00 p.m.
8th grade	10:30 p.m.
9th grade	11:00-11:30 p.m.
10th grade	11:30 p.m.-12:00 a.m.
11th grade	12:00-12:30 a.m.
12th grade	12:30-1:00 a.m.

As The Parent Of A Teenager Hosting A Party

Follow the same procedures suggested when your teenager is having a few friends over, with a few additions.

- Keep parties small and manageable — 20-25 teenagers per adult couple.

- Encourage "by invitation only" activities. Determine how party-crashers will be handled and by whom.

- Agree that guests who leave may not return. Agree to other rules such as lights being left on, rooms in the house which are off limits, etc. Be aware of hidden alcohol — behind a bush in backyard, etc.

Money

Lack of money to purchase alcohol or other drugs generally doesn't inhibit the abuser or the dedicated drug user. If necessary, he or she will steal to support the drug habit — from parents, employers, friends, etc. Limited funds, however, do seem to deter the experimenter and the recreational user. "I'm broke" is usually an acceptable excuse to the peer group.

Available money supply may consist of an allowance, cash gifts, and earnings. You can help your teenager establish realistic spending priorities, so that booze, pot, etc., if on it, are near the bottom of the priority list.

- Teenagers should be taught their money isn't just for immediate pleasures such as "partying," with the responsibility for necessities going to someone else. Establish what necessities are.

- Parents need to know how much money a teenager has available and how it is being spent. Consider requiring your teenager to keep a simple expense ledger. If he or she is responsible, consider a checking account.

- If you provide an allowance, clearly establish what it is for. Consider making funds provided for a specific use available in a lump sum, to be drawn on only for that purpose, rather than making it part of the weekly allowance.

- Encourage cash gifts to be saved and/or designated for something special, rather than used indiscriminately for "walking around money."

ALTERNATE ACTIVITIES

One way to combat undesirable "hangin' out," beer parties, etc. is to vigorously promote imaginative alternative activities. The key to a successful, long-term program of alternatives is to encourage and pattern a child from *early* adolescence toward appropriate, challenging and fun outside activities. Include their friends and assist them in arranging transportation and financing. Older teenagers tell us their main criteria for ranking outside activities are: Does it sound like fun? How much does it cost? Who else is going? How do I get there and back, and how much will *that* cost?

They also warn us that once teenagers have accepted alcohol and marijuana use as their social norm, they are likely to relate their drug of choice to *any* unsupervised social activity. For example, splitting a six-pack in the theatre parking lot before a movie, sharing a joint on the ski-lift, etc. Our teenage advisors also pointed out that party time is usually Friday and Saturday *nights*, and that daytime activities won't counter the problem.

Listed below are some available alternative activities for you to consider.

- School sponsored activities. (Look at your school's student handbook.)

Active participation in sports • Spectator sports and events • School dances and parties • Special interest clubs and activities

- Sports and physical activities outside of school.

  Snow skiing • Swimming, waterskiing, etc. • Horseback riding • Bowling • Golf and driving range • Tennis • Volleyball • Badminton • Trampolining • Bicycling • Skating (ice or roller) • Jogging • Fishing • Hiking, climbing, camping • Hunting • Judo and karate • Handball • Touch football • Body building • Sports recreational leagues • Dance (all kinds) • Community centers • Girls/Boys Clubs of America • YMCA/YWCA youth activities

NOTE: A concern about physical fitness often discourages drug use.

- Whatever your religious convictions and preferences, do consider that many churches, synagogues and temples have excellent youth groups with a wide variety of activities available. You and your son or daughter may not need to be members or even attend services for him or her to participate. Young Life, for example, a Christian sponsored organization for high school students, is open to *any* young person, regardless of faith.

- Recreation and entertainment.

  Movies ($1 nights) • Shopping malls • Sports Centers • Plays • Amusement parks • Putt-putt golf • Concerts • Circuses, fairs, carnivals • Water World • Spectator sports • Rodeos • Teen clubs • A night of Trivial Pursuit, Backgammon, cards, etc.

NOTE: Personal interests or hobbies including art, music and dance often serve as forms of recreation and entertainment.

- Sightseeing in and around major cities. (Pick up a tourist guide. Also, many museums are listed in the phone book under "Museum.")

  > Zoo • Botanic gardens • Museums of natural history • Planetariums • Factory tours • Historic sites

- Family activities should also be considered alternatives. Each member might take turns in planning the activity, taking a guest, etc. You may be rewarded with, "Gee, Mom/Dad, this *is* more fun than just hanging around. Maybe I'll do this with my friends next weekend."

- Join together with other parents, interested teachers and coaches, and other concerned community members to form an alternative activities group, which will sponsor activities to compete with beer and keg parties. This has been very successful in Fort Collins, Colorado for several years, which proves that teenagers *will* go to a non-alcoholic party — if they feel they can't afford to pass it up.

  Sample Activities:

  > Soc hops • Open houses after games and events • New Year's party • Theme party (Valentine, etc.) • Hayride and barbecue • Fundraisers (carwashes, fun run) • Block party • Swimming party

A community task force in the Metro-Denver area felt that a separately designated "alternative activities student group," would be labeled as "not cool" in their school community. Thus, they formed a "Community Activity Boosters" parent group designed to lend assistance and support (money, food, chaperones, ideas, etc.) to the customary student-sponsored school social activities. By enhancing and facilitating existing social activities which are school- sponsored and student-directed, the group is attracting a larger and larger segment of the student body into alcohol and drug-free alternatives.

LETTING GO

By high school graduation, young people should have reached reasonable autonomy and be able to stand on their own the majority of the time — emotionally, intellectually and financially. Mainly, they should be capable of being in charge of their own lives and making adult decisions with confidence and pride. The only way for this to be accomplished is for the child to actively disengage, and the parent to gradually let go.

Conflict during this normal adolescent "breaking-away" period is often caused by parents who demand blind obedience and refuse to allow the teenagers to think for themselves. A normal adolescent, most often, will react to this with anger, resentment, open rebellion and even a desire for revenge. The latter may account for some teenagers' early drug use.

Adolescence may be a more painful trauma for parents than for adolescents, because parenting styles are an important part of the adult identity. It needn't be if parents can realize that the problem of letting the kids grow up just necessitates a redefining of the way parents express their love and concern.

- Acknowledge your teenager as an emerging man or woman with unique individuality, who has the right to make choices within certain predetermined limits. Teenagers have a right to their own feelings and opinions.

- Resist the temptation to live your life through your children. Don't burden *them* with the responsibility of establishing *your* identity, security and sense of value.

- Recognize that your adolescent may temporarily, or even permanently, reject some of your outmoded values. Listen to his or her justification.

- Try to operate on a rational level. Recognizing one's own motivation in dealings with their teenager is what distinguishes parents who can handle their child's adolescence from those who can't.

- Reinforce and encourage your teenagers to employ for themselves the basic principles of good decision-making. State the problem. Identify the options. Weigh the pluses and minuses (consequences) of each. Then choose one and go for it.

Constructively support their choices.

Give your teenagers room to fail.

Help them learn from their mistakes without criticizing them or saying, "I told you so."

Be available for emergency back-up when a young person makes the wrong decision, but don't constantly charge to the rescue.

- Encourage your teenagers to develop effective coping strategies and to consistently use them to confront confusing or unpleasant issues. Advise them that there are limitless possibilities for problem solving. But let any involvement on your part be part of the solution and not part of the problem.

- The adolescent no longer needs as much nurturing and attention to his physical comforts. The sooner parents insist that he take over the most basic functions of physical care, the sooner the adolescent begins to see himself as competent in other areas.

- Inspire further competency and confidence by requiring your teenager to assume some type of fiscal responsibility and accountability. Let *him* find the best buy and make arrangements to pay for it.

- Constantly emphasize in word and deed that your love is *unconditional.* Praise him when he handles a situation well. When he blows it, give him credit for trying and let him try again.

- Recognize that your teenager is breaking away from you as a child and try to reconnect with him or her on an adult level. Share your self. Let your son or daughter see you as a person who is aware and open about your own past and present hang-ups, problems, etc.

CREATING A PERSONAL CHALLENGE FOR THE ADOLESCENT*

Never in the history of the United States has society given a generation so much and asked so little in return. And many young people would respond: that is part of the problem.

Yet if caring and concern is measured by what is asked as well as by what is given, society has not served this generation of Americans as generously as it seems. What's missing? Skeptical adults would be surprised by the answer from scores of young people: the lack of challenging responsibilities against which they can shape their characters, their values and their commitment to society.

Ralph W. Larkin, a New York City social science consultant and author of papers and books on the youth culture, perceives a hidden despair in the children of the '80s. The country is "still producing a similar young person to that of the '60s and '70s. They're not that different," he said.

But Larkin adds that "the further you get from the '60s, the harder it is for kids to envision any alternatives. They are still plagued by the senselessness of much of what they do. Going to school seems senseless. They see themselves as engaging in meaningless activity which leads to more meaningless activity. But since this is 1981, there's no alternative to it, no dissident youth culture. So they compromise. They participate without commitment."

Probably never before in history has a generation been so well shielded from society's harsh economic realities. The starkest conditions of poverty and hunger are far removed from the experience of middle-class suburban kids.

Generous allowances and a dramatic expansion of jobs suited to the part-time employment of teen-agers in the food service and retail businesses in the 1970s have put more money in the pockets of these young people for cars, stereos, fashions and even drugs, than at any time in the past.

And their boredom seems connected to this irony: children who have been given so much, many of them at least, have been denied what their parents experienced — meaningful struggle, work which gives a sense of purpose, even sacrifice, which makes one feel needed by others.

---

*Excerpt with permission from Dan Morgan "Young Americans Searching for Something of Their 'Own'." *Washington Post*

What's going on here? A wealthy and dynamic country gives young people extraordinary benefits and opportunities and the children respond by feeling bored or, worse still, oppressed. The bewilderment of parents was summarized by a black father who himself struggled out of a background of rural poverty to reach the suburban middle class. He couldn't understand his own son's lack of motivation at school.

But a friend offered an intriguing answer:

"Perhaps he has not had your advantages."

In other words, is it possible that the very struggle of overcoming disadvantages, the work and discipline and sense of goals, is what's missing for so many of today's young people? A growing list of experts think so.

A private committee that made a national study of the pros and cons of a system of civilian service concluded in 1979 that "little is asked of young people except that they be consumers of goods and services. . . . A vast industry serves youth with schooling, entertainment, and goods of all kinds, but there are limited opportunities for the young themselves to produce goods and serve others."

5.
Intervention

WHERE DOES INTERVENTION BEGIN?

At School?

A comprehensive and clearly-worded substance abuse policy can be a very effective weapon in a school system's war on student drug abuse. However, the degree of effectiveness is largely determined by the level of enforcement that is supported by school administration, parents and the community at large. In Colorado, the Cherry Creek School District developed its "Substance Abuse Policy and Procedure" with the assistance of a specially appointed task force which was composed of not only educators, but also students, parents and key members of the community. The policy is effective within school district jurisdiction. A student is within the school district's jurisdiction when on school grounds, at school-sanctioned activities, in vehicles dispatched by the district, and at school bus stops.

Students shall be subject to disciplinary action for being under the influence of, using, distributing, selling, storing in cars or lockers, giving or exchanging controlled substances, drug paraphernalia or counterfeit drugs. Suspension will occur when a student is involved in any way with drugs or alcohol. If a student continues to ignore this policy, expulsion could result. The entire policy and procedure appears in Appendix J.

Dr. Donald K. Goe, Deputy Superintendent of the Cherry Creek School District, has emphasized that schools should aid only in *identifying* children involved in substance abuse. Treatment, he feels, belongs in the hands of professionals. The motivating purpose of suspension, therefore, is to facilitate a conference between parents and school personnel in order to deal with the situation. Once conditions which have led to the problem are dealt with, suspension can be overruled. The Substance Abuse Policy and Procedure, in other words, is intended to move the situation into a corrective mode. Discipline is secondary.

Although this policy and procedure is in force in each school building within the Cherry Creek School District, the specific interpretation and implementation is done at the local level by the building principal. Such implementation might include:

- In-service training to educate teachers about symptoms of drug use impacting a student's school performance and about ways to deal effectively with a student suspected of drug use.
- Designating a specific person within the school (e.g., the school nurse) who will serve as a resource and contact for students, faculty and parents. Providing such contact with appropriate drug education and a current resource list.
- Establishing an effective student drug prevention curriculum.
- Developing a system to enhance parent awareness and education.
- Setting up a procedure for reporting and handling *suspected* drug users. (Such a procedure is often difficult to implement because teachers and administrators want to avoid the risk of a parental lawsuit.)
- Forming an optional aftercare support group for students who have been in treatment centers and/or are undergoing other forms of treatment.
- Forming qualified intervention teams of teachers, counselors and coaches.
- Supporting community drug and alcohol task force groups, related parent programs, student-directed programs to discourage drinking and driving, student groups concerned about drug abuse in general, etc.

At Home?

Many teenagers who use alcohol, marijuana and/or other drugs do so outside of school and supervised school activities. Weekend use is particularly prevalent. Thus, parents should be aware of their child's use of chemical substances before it occurs at school. However, many parents are inclined to deny their teenager's drug involvement until trouble at school forces them to acknowledge it.

Once parents have determined their teenager is involved in some way with illegal substances, they must assess the extent of use. Is he or she an experimenter, a user or an abuser? Has addiction developed? This investigative process may entail talking with the teenager's friends, other parents, teachers, counselors, etc. and even searching through the teenager's room, car and personal effects.

The latter is often traumatic for parents because of their concern for a child's right to privacy and trust. Yet, a search under these circumstances is warranted when considered as a diagnostic tool — like an x-ray. The potential health risks involved in letting uncurbed drug abuse get further out of control are too great to let protocol deter diagnostic investigation.

Once drug use is established, it is clearly the parents' responsibility to intervene. The intervention may only necessitate taking a hard line at home, or it may lead to counselling or inpatient drug therapy. If parents do not intervene, the use may progress to a point where it is destructive, not only to the teenager, but to the entire family as well. Another motivating factor to consider is that parents may be held legally responsible for the actions of their teenage drinker or drug user. One unfortunate incident resulting in a civil action could potentially wipe out a family financially.

WHEN AND HOW DOES USE BECOME ABUSE — THEN WHAT?

There is some confusion among laypeople about what constitutes "use" and what constitutes "abuse." For example, is a teenager who uses pot or cocaine (illegal drugs) every now and then *or* a 17-year-old who uses alcohol (a legal drug) moderately, but illegally, labeled an abuser or just a criminal user? Actually both situations are considered abuse, even though they may not fall into the category of abuse as shown in the pyramid.

Most medical experts define abuse as the misuse of any substance. Under that definition, the use of an *illegal* substance is abuse even on a onetime basis. Likewise, the inappropriate use of legal substances such as alcohol and prescribed medication is considered abuse. Abuse is also referred to as substance use which causes physical, mental, or emotional impairment. Therefore, the teenager's use of *any* drug (other than nicotine, caffeine, prescribed drugs, and legitimate medicinal use of over-the-counter drugs) is commonly referred to as "teenage drug abuse."

This boggles the mind of many parents, who don't want to call their teenage "partier" a drug abuser. They prefer to use the terms "experimenter," "user" and "abuser," to refer to the "stages" of adolescent chemical use. A chart outlining the stages of adolescent drug abuse appears in Appendix D. Below is a frequency of drug use pyramid to assist a parent in putting teenage behavior with illegal substances into their perspective using their terminology.

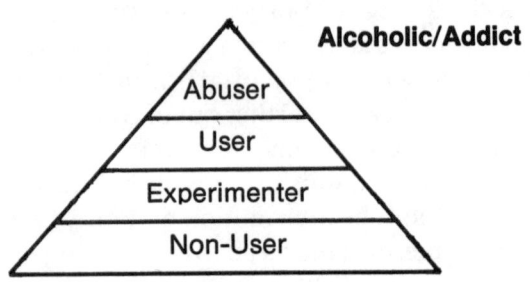

Alcoholic/Addict
- Abuser
- User
- Experimenter
- Non-User

Non-user — A non-user does not use alcohol or drugs at all — period. The majority of our elementary school children fit into this category.

Experimenter — Adolescents, by their very nature, are curious and are inclined to experiment with many things, including alcohol and drugs. They want to find out how it affects them and how others will react. Part of their high is derived from acting grown up and defying parents. There are at least 3 categories of experimenters:

- Some children will try it a few times for the thrill, not care for it particularly and soon return to non-user status.

- Other children may also try it and not like it. Yet, they keep on experimenting due to peer pressure or other motivating factors until they are ready to join the ranks of the "users."

- Still other adolescents who try it LIKE IT. They begin to develop tolerance — the more they take of the drug, the less effect they get from each dose. Gradually, they may begin to use the drug more regularly and more heavily. However, some of these eager experimenters may "experiment" only once or twice and then, almost immediately, become enthusiastic users, or abusers or even an addicts. Reportedly, the latter has been found true often in "crack" experimentation, although it has been encountered with other substances as well.

User — "Use" is a broad general term meaning the voluntary taking of substances in any form for curiosity, pleasure, self-medication (to reduce tension or pain) or to escape from unpleasant environment, conflicts or feelings.

- Some teenagers will continue experimental use by occasionally drinking beer and/or smoking pot. This is usually done on weekends or during the summer — and mostly with friends. These teenagers, at this point, can take it or leave it alone. It's no big deal to them either way. This type of experimenter, sometimes called a recreational user, is compared to the adult social drinker who drinks occasionally at cocktail parties.

- The more regular teenage user "parties" (or uses) almost every weekend. Indeed, he or she may even get stoned or just plain drunk from time to time. Some teenagers, at this point, begin to experiment occasionally with harder drugs like cocaine. Teenager users may confine themselves to weekend use indefinitely or until they get into trouble (e.g., a DUI or a possession charge) and begin to seriously examine the risk/reward relationship. Or perhaps, their parents force the issue.

Abuser — But the adolescent may, instead, progress gradually into even more regular use, which begins to border on preoccupation. This may include:

- Getting drunk or stoned every weekend. The attitude may be "weekends are made for getting 'blasted.'"

- Waking up on Monday morning and immediately anticipating next weekend.

- Moving the "beginning of the weekend" back to Thursday, then Wednesday, etc.

- Considering school afternoons or evenings as a weekend and suitable for a party or weekend type "hanging out."

- Rationalizing solitary drinking/drug use, exhibiting early "signs and symptoms" of alcoholism/addiction (see Appendix C), and using more hard drugs.

- At some point, the teenager may view life as an endless series of back-to-back weekends. The chemical substances will be used any time any place — on weekends, during the week, at work, before school, after school and during school. When it reaches this point, use becomes fairly apparent and a chemical dependency problem may have developed. The school may eventually catch up with the student, but many teenage substance abusers are very clever and/or devious about their use. If the parent has not picked up on the problem, the school may not either.

Alcoholic/Addict — A very heavy teenage abuser may not necessarily be an "addict" or "alcoholic" if he or she can discontinue use at will. An addict's misuse, or abuse, of a drug is uncontrollable, regardless of the known consequences. "Addiction" is dependency and almost invariably has both physiological and psychological components. Human addiction is not necessarily determined by impairment, although addiction is considered a disease (e.g., alcoholism). Rather, it is usually diagnosed when the user has a continuing craving and physical need for a substance, the user requires increasing amounts of the substance to obtain the same effect, and the user experiences symptoms of withdrawal when the substance is discontinued. New findings demonstrate many users of crack meet these criteria (dependence, tolerance and withdrawal) after a few minutes or hours of crack use. In some cases, other substances may be almost instantly addictive.

"RED FLAGS" OF ADOLESCENT DRUG INVOLVEMENT*

Drug Peer Group

Who do your children associate with? How do their friends fit into the "symptoms" list? We all know that, whether we want to admit it or not, peer influences are the primary predictor of an adolescent's lifestyle and frame of reference. *You can influence your children's peer group!*

Changes in Behavior

Adolescents are normally in a constant state of change. The "changes as symptoms" are different. These changes are defined

---

*Reprinted with permission of Mr. Tom Brewster, Associate Director, Addiction Research and Treatment Services, University of Colorado Health Sciences Center

as dramatic alterations in behavior or mood, such as a change from being open to secretive, loud to quiet, happy to depressed, energetic to listless, etc.

Loss of Interest in Normal Activities

"Normal activities" include those hobbies or social activities which the adolescent has characteristically enjoyed. If there is a sudden loss of interest in activities that have normally been of interest, pay attention!

Changed Physical Appearance

Significant weight loss or gain should not go unattended. Loss of skin color or "just looking sick" are also warning signals.

Drug Paraphernalia

People who use drugs may own a wide variety of items, called drug paraphernalia, designed for drug use, be it to smoke a marijuana cigarette, snort cocaine, or inject heroin. If you find such items, check out the situation!

Isolation from the Family

The adolescent who becomes withdrawn, sullen, secretive, who receives phone calls at odd hours, begins seeing friends whom you don't know, and who basically isolates himself, is exhibiting unusual behavior which should be addressed.

Poor School Performance

Drug use is almost always accompanied by deterioration in school performance. This includes tardiness, absences, poor grades, changed peer group, changed attitudes toward school.

Loss of Parental Control

Although it is healthy for adolescents to reject authority while stressing their independence, it is not healthy for the parents to lose control. If your child is attempting to negate your control, pay attention!

Drug Vocabulary

Use of words that denote drug involvement, or "street talk," might be an indication of a new antisocial peer group influence. Keep an "ear" on what your child says.

Drug Availability

Parents who drink alcoholic beverages, or use other drugs (marijuana), sometimes make these substances available around the house. Although it is difficult and possibly inadvisable to hide alcoholic drinks, parents must make sure that they are not making a drug available to their children.

—— ADOLESCENT PROBLEM DRINKERS —— COMPARED TO OTHER ADOLESCENTS

In a study* of the development of problem behavior in youth, it was found that the characteristics listed below are significantly related to an adolescent's transition from abstainer to drinker.

Factors Relating To Parents

- Parents are less involved with them.
- Parents are less positive and affectionate.
- The teenagers value self-determination and autonomy from parents.
- They feel less parental disapproval for their drinking.
- The parents themselves are heavier drinkers.
- They sense a wider discrepancy between expectations of parents and expectations of peers.

Factors Relating To Peers

- They feel more influenced by peers than by parents.
- They have more peers who model problem drinking and other problem behavior.
- They receive more peer approval of their drinking.

---

*Results of this study were first reported by the National Institute on Alcohol Abuse and Alcoholism in the Fourth Special Report to the U.S. Congress on Alcohol and Health.

Factors Relating To Academics

- They place a lower value on academic achievement.
- They expect less academic success.

Miscellaneous Factors

- They are more tolerant of deviance.
- They attach less importance to religion.
- They value the positive aspects of drinking as outweighing the negative aspects.

EXPERIMENTATION SUGGESTED ACTIONS

Unfortunately, preventive parenting isn't always 100% effective. Even though "a family is healthy and there is a good relationship between parent and child based on love and bondage," says Tom Brewster, Associate Director of the Addiction Research and Treatment Service, University of Colorado Health Sciences Center, "the relationship will not always be perfect. The adolescent may still want to experiment with drugs, check things out and rebel." Once a parent discovers his child is experimenting with drugs a number of approaches can be implemented to handle the situation effectively. Parents have the power *and* the responsibility to intercede in their children's use and abuse of drugs. However, they need confidence and assertiveness to change their children's behavior.

According to Brewster, there are no universal recipes for how a family should handle one of its members becoming involved with drugs. The following suggestions are only possible approaches.

✔ *Accept The Possibility* — Even though all signs point to it, it's tough to accept that your teenager may be using drugs. Most kids experiment from time to time. Don Shaw, Coordinator for Health Education in the Jefferson County schools in Colorado, says girls will experiment more in 8th grade than any other year. Boys, on the other hand, experiment more during their sophomore year. When half of all high school students drink at least once a month, and a somewhat smaller percentage use pot at least once a month, the odds are that your teenager is one of them. Even though experimentation might earmark healthy development, it can also lead to abuse, psychological and family problems, etc.

✔ *Open Communication* — Families frequently find themselves operating on a crisis basis, i.e., management by crisis. This is a reactive form of functioning and usually occurs because there is normally limited communication going on. Thus, when an issue like drug experimentation comes up, it's a crisis. Therefore, it's important to discuss your concern early on, to not hide it or worry about it alone.

✔ *Confront The Issue* — Sure it's hard to do, but someone has to start doing something and the best way is to open the issue up to discussion. This can be handled between the parents, between the involved child and one or both parents, or with the whole family. The point is, do something!

DISCUSSION GUIDELINES

Be flexible when you approach your teenager. Understand that he (or she) will be uncomfortable and possibly rebellious when the subject of drugs is broached. Unless you have concrete evidence, do not accuse him, but rather let him know you're concerned. Accusations often result in denial. Talk about your personal concern for him. Try to keep the discussion on a rational level. Overly emotional, angry outbursts, labeling and name calling serve only to cut off parent-child communication prematurely. The purpose of the discussion is to deal with his *behavior* and not his *character!* You want him to know that even if you disapprove of his actions, you still love him.

When The Parent Initiates An Exploratory Discussion

Create an opportunity for an open-ended dialogue with your teenager. Break down communication barriers and discuss the subject of experimentation. Here are a few ideas which may stimulate your own ideas about how to begin such a conversation.

OBJECTIVE: To express concern without accusation.

"I hear so many things about different kids at school.

INTERVENTION | 109

Sometimes I worry about you and your friends being under so much pressure. It must be a real challenge for you not to be tempted to. . ."

"The paper and TV news report on so many tragedies involving teenagers and alcohol and drugs. It tears me up to even think about something like that happening to you and your friends. I don't want to spoil your good time, but I am always terribly concerned about your safety. I don't want you killed in some senseless tragedy. I love you too much!"

OBJECTIVE: To let your teenagers know you will always stand by to support them and their friends, even if you do not condone the situation. To encourage them to resume acting responsibly even though they may have already committed an irresponsible act.

"I don't want you to get drunk or stoned or hang around with kids who do. You know I don't approve of it and why. But I do realize something unforeseen *could* happen. If it should, don't panic. Call me to come get you or take a cab home. There's always $20.00 under the blue vase."

"Please call me if there is a problem with one of your friends. I wouldn't want anything to happen to any of them."

"You have been responsible with _____ in the past, and I would therefore expect responsibility about _____ now. If you make a mistake, let's fix it right then, rather than compound it."

OBJECTIVE: To encourage your teenagers to see the situation from other perspectives which helps them to use empathy and consideration in weighing the issue.

"I feel sorry for kids whose parent(s) have alcohol and other kinds of drug problems. What would you think if I were to come home stoned or drunk? It is terrifying to see someone you love staggering, incoherent, violently ill or just plain nasty and mean."

"I feel so sorry for that poor kid who. . . . How would you feel if you were "out of it" and seriously injured or killed somebody?"

NOTE: A rigid or autocratic stance will often cause a normal adolescent to be rebellious and react with negative behavior (act out).

When Your Child Initiates An Exploratory Discussion*

Scenario: Your teenager informs you that a peer is experimenting with pot and that he has asked your child to join. What do you do?

- Get as much information as you can, matter-of-factly, without resorting to a third-degree police grilling. Avoid accusing your teenager of participating, but keep in mind that *he may have done so.* Don't be immediately judgmental and/or uncharitable toward your youngster's friends. If you act immediately suspicious, you might block further communication on the subject. Do not panic or overact! Your child may be doing all right. The fact that he has approached you with this information is a positive sign. Reinforce your teenager's willingness to talk to you about the subject.

- Pay attention to your own feelings as you listen. Are you scared? Puzzled? Angry? Sad? It is usually, but not always, helpful to hold back your own feelings until 1) you understand fully what your child is saying and feeling, and 2) until you can think through how you want to express your own feelings and thoughts. Right now he (or she) needs to know you care, and you are interested in understanding what happened and his or her *feelings* about it.

- While you listen, try to figure out *why* your child is telling you this. There could be several possible reasons.

    Your child fears his own lack of self-control and wants you to set limits.

    Your child needs more information about the effects or consequences of smoking pot.

    Your child does not feel a need to experiment. He simply wants your support for a limit he has already established for himself.

---

*Source material for this topic was developed by: CAP Task Force, Kenneth H. Ash, M.D. and Armon Johannsen, Fort Collins, Colorado

INTERVENTION | 111

Your child doesn't want to join in but is afraid to stand up to the friends. He wants help in dealing with peer pressure.

Your child has already dealt very effectively with the situation and wants you to know so you can give him the much needed pat-on-the-back.

- Before giving your advice, limits, etc., find out what your child is planning to do about the problem. Have him or her weigh the positive and negative aspects of each action being considered and discuss how to deal with possible consequences.

- Decide your own position. Now that you have carefully and patiently listened to your youngster *and* your own thoughts and feelings, you are in the best position to decide what you want or need to do next. For example, you may decide that:

    Your teenager has the situation under control and plans to do the best thing. Therefore, all you want to do is reinforce his good judgment and maturity.

    Your teenager has several blind spots or is misinformed in several areas. Therefore, you will tell him what you know or suggest what he can do to fill the gaps in knowledge.

    You think that an alternative action is better than the one your youngster has chosen. You may feel specific things are necessary to remedy the situation. Therefore, you will want to respectfully tell him so and why.

    You feel strongly that the course of action your child is planning is unacceptable to you. Therefore, you must tell him that you can't allow it and why.

    You as the parent feel an immediate need to set certain limits or lay down specific consequences.

- Whether your intervention is the pleasurable one of telling your child you respect his decision or the unpleasant one of setting and dealing out consequences for undesirable behavior, you will probably want to do the following:

    Be very clear and specific about what you think and feel and how you arrived at those conclusions.

    Express clearly your own expectations concerning what the youngster will do, with whom, and when.

Let your teenager know that you are available to help in any way that he or she deems appropriate. This might include helping him rehearse saying "no" or your talking with the friend in question. Take a look at the "For Kids Only" section of this book.

Make sure that your youngster fully understands the consequences and limits you will impose for specified unacceptable behavior.

DEALING WITH THE "RECREATIONAL USER"

A high percentage of the underage teenagers in the United States are social or recreational users of alcohol and/or marijuana. If and when you find that your own teenager is one of them, dealing with this knowledge can be "mind-boggling."

You are concerned and disappointed that your child has advanced beyond the "curious" experimental stage. Yet, you are relieved he (or she) is just a recreational/social user and doesn't consistently get drunk or stoned. You may choose to recognize the recreational use as just a phase adolescents go through. Yet, you realize it's a very dangerous phase — one which might end abruptly because of an accidental overdose or a drunk driving fatality. He may survive it, but be permanently crippled — physically, mentally or emotionally. You wonder if, due to some wild prank, he might foolishly pick up a cumbersome police record to follow him through life. You also admit that any degree of illegal drug use is a crime punishable under the law, and that even alcohol is considered an illegal drug for an underage teen.

If the tip-off to your teenager's recreational use was seeing the youngster come home stoned or drunk, you should probably be asking yourself if this is really just experimental social use, or if it is a sign of something more advanced. (Look at the Awareness Test for Parents in Appendix B.) Likewise, you could ask yourself if the teenager, consciously or subconsciously, might have set himself up to get caught as a way of indirectly asking you for specific limits to help him deal with the tremendous peer pressure he is facing.

Most parents acknowledge that the teenage social alcohol/drug scene is so widespread that they can't reasonably and effectively isolate or totally remove their teenager. WHAT DO YOU DO?

First, take a look at a few of your options.

- ✔ Do nothing. Keep your fingers crossed and just hope that your son or daughter does not experience any serious repercussions.

- ✔ Demand unconditionally that he or she immediately stop recreational use, threaten severe punishment for disobedience and follow through. This *may* effectively solve the problem, or it may just alert your teenager to proceed with more caution. Only constant parental supervision, a breath test or urinalysis can ascertain whether the teenager is continuing to use the drug — unless the youngster comes home obviously high or smelling of alcohol or marijuana.

- ✔ Accept the fact that your teenager is currently a recreational user and that you probably can't always effectively monitor whether he (or she) is using a drug socially. Without condoning his illegal actions (which are also irresponsible), stress the basic principles of responsible use: Be aware of and stay within your limit. Don't drink and drive. Don't combine alcohol with marijuana. When the teenager uses substances irresponsibly — and you catch him — retaliate with *heavy* penalties. This approach is used most often by parents whose teenagers are using alcohol only.

Before you decide on one of the above or any other option, a discussion with your teenager is in order. Remember the principles of good communication, and don't hold the conversation when he or she is in any way under the influence. Neither do you want your teen in a defensive mood. Your goal is to promote open, honest, two-way communication about a very sensitive subject.

You might initially set an upbeat mood by telling your teenager how positively you perceive him as a person, his good points, what he has going for him, etc. Stress the positive! *Then*, describe the "party" problem as you see it and encourage him to share with you how he sees it. Bert Singleton, Executive Director of Big Brothers, Inc. in Denver, suggests some other points you might consider. These points are helpful in dealing with any stage of user/experimenter.

- • In bringing about a behavior change, start from an initial point of agreement. You must have a common ground to work from, so you don't establish an adversarial relationship.

- In prompting a behavior change, be careful not to increase your child's fear, anxiety, anger, etc. Acute anxiety causes adolescents to shut down the logical learning process. An angry or frightened teenager not only refuses to hear what you are saying, but could also increase the drug process.

- In order to change, one needs an active support system. Friends, family, and neighbors need to be there for the teenager or else no change will come about. Too often, support at home is negative and therefore inhibits progress.

- Bringing about change is more effective if the change is additive. Add something to your teenager's life before taking something away. For example, at the same time you are urging him to drastically restructure his social life, encourage him to pursue a challenging new interest (e.g., sports, guitar, dance, karate, etc.)

- Set small intermediate goals that are attainable.

- It is easier to initiate change than it is to sustain it. The key is maintaining the change. Build reinforcement and check points into a long-term plan.

- When discussing the pros and cons of drug use with your teenager, present both sides: their side with the benefits first, then your side with the negatives. Remain open minded and let your child know you understand there are viewpoints other than yours.

- Reward the teenager for making an effort to change. Altering behavior patterns is extremely difficult and requires careful nurturing. This process is initially enhanced with rewards from the parents. Then, as the teenager progresses, he will begin to get rewards from the behavior change itself.

- Look for the triggers that pull the teenager into drug use. A certain friend? A particular situation?

- Make changes in the regular schedule to break up habits. For example, if an adult always smokes while watching TV in his favorite chair, he should watch TV sitting on the couch as part of his "quit-smoking" campaign. If your teenager is having problems dealing with the weekend party scene, organize some compelling family activities which will offer positive distraction on weekends.

- A person needs specific reasons to motivate themselves to break out of a pattern. You can only create an environment conducive to change. You cannot *make* someone change. They have to want this for themselves.

- Adolescents should be able to view their parents as allies. Parents and teenagers need to work on problems together. Thus, the adolescent needs to see that the parents want to change some of their less desirable habits and traits, too.

- Understand adolescence is a time of pulling away. Parents can win the battle for control and eventually will, but this prevents the adolescent from accomplishing a necessary function of adolescence — breaking away from the parents as a child and reconnecting with them on an adult level. Parents can win the battle, but lose the war.

A LOOK AT THE MORE ADVANCED USER

Scenario: Matt is a 15-year-old sophomore. His best friend has been expelled because marijuana was found in both his car and locker. Matt is getting D's and F's when presumably he can earn A's and B's. He has dropped out of track and other school activities. These facts plus certain other evidence suggest that Matt is involved with drugs.

Matt's parents have forbidden him to be around his best friend after school and weekends. The friend's parents have been notified that until he straightens out, Matt is not allowed to see him. Matt, a dedicated rock fan, has also been told that if his grades don't improve by mid-term, he will lose his favorite tapes.

What Are The Chances Of Matt Straightening Up?

The outcome can't be reasonably predicted because the fact pattern in the scenario does not specify the "other evidence" of drug use. Therefore, it is unclear how deeply Matt may be involved in drugs at this point. The parents have exercised their prerogative to intercede. If the problem isn't too advanced, and they have the confidence to tackle the issue, an assertive, no-nonsense approach may well change Matt's behavior.

Parental action may often bring about a temporary improvement in a drug user's school performance. In some cases though, cheating is a large part of the improvement. Temporary behavior changes, unfortunately, often satisfy the parents, who then prematurely relax their tough, no-nonsense stance. Without consistent intervention, the drug abuse continues to progress to more advanced stages and could very possibly become addiction.

Many factors might cause Matt's parents to prematurely consider the situation under control. Presumably, Matt is aware of exactly why his parents suspect he is using drugs. This knowledge could motivate him to be more devious about his drug use, rather than to stop it altogether. Unless the parents are knowledgeable about paraphernalia and the more subtle signs and symptoms of adolescent drug use (see Appendix C and D), Matt could conceivably succeed in concealing his continued drug use for a time.

Let's examine the parents' decision to separate Matt from his best friend. Robert L. DuPont, M. D., former Director of the National Institute on Drug Abuse (NIDA) has been quoted as saying, "The single main determinant of whether a particular young person uses drugs like marijuana is whether or not his best friend uses it." Although Matt's parents have made it difficult for him to spend time with his friend, it is not impossible. For example: "Oh, I ran into him at the mall. I couldn't very well just walk away. He's such a wimp! You guys were right." The parents are manipulated by Matt's negative remarks about his friend and gradually slacken the rigidity of the enforced separation. Or, Matt may really drop the friend in question, and then surreptitiously seek out new friends who are drug users.

The bottom line is that Matt's parents are traveling a road littered with misleading detour signs, none of which lead to their ultimate goal — straightening Matt out. They are concerned and conscientiously try to confront the problem. However, they must be willing to do whatever it takes for as long as it takes. Matt must realize that his parents aren't kidding: his carefully plotted cons will be ineffectual, and his parents are willing to take any steps necessary to resolve his drug abuse problem satisfactorily. Under the circumstances, the parents might do well to consult their family physician or pediatrician. They themselves may need outside support to accomplish their goal.

Set Limits — Act Instead Of React

When drug use is undeniably evident, or many of the symptoms seem to be present, restate your position and make absolutely clear the limits you are prepared to enact. Remember, parents have both the right and the responsibility to take a position! ("I love you too much to let you ruin or even end your life at 15.") Make certain you are prepared to follow through with the consequences you establish. Empty threats are meaningless. It is also extremely important to enforce limits with fairness and consistency. Be aware, however, of problems involved in enforcement.

- If you forbid your teenager to associate with a certain person you must:

    Express clearly how you came to your conclusion.

    Be prepared to keep track of his or her every waking moment by being home before and after school and providing supervision at all times.

    Be prepared for anger and resentment on the part of the teenager.

    Teenagers usually choose friends who complement the attitudes and values they already have. Hence, if your teen chooses a friend who has undesirable traits, you as a parent may need to examine your own teenager's values.

- Most children will change their behavior after a loss of privileges, but some do not. If you suspect drug use because of your child's poor school performance or other "red flags," you may want to set certain limits which give more structure to your child's life, to help him improve school performance and avoid undesirable friends and peer groups. This type of limit setting tells teenagers what they can and cannot do and when they must do it.

Contingency Contracts As A Method Of Enforcement

For teenagers with more advanced problems in drug use, some parents set up a written contingency contract. The contract states that if the child doesn't meet assigned and accepted responsibility he or she loses predetermined rights, privileges, etc. Once the agreement has been made and written down, the contract is signed by both parents and teenager. In effect, a contract says, "If you use drugs (or miss your curfew, etc.), this is what we'll do." When you know what is important to your teenager, you can use those items or privileges as disciplinary tools for intervention and prevention.

For example, if a contract is broken the teenager agrees beforehand to:

- Give a favorite item to charity (e.g., a cassette or video tape, hair dryer, tape deck, radio, skis, etc.).
- Give up use of the car for an agreed upon period of time.
- Cut off telephone and/or TV privileges for a specified period.

A sample contract appears in Appendix I. However, before parents draw up a severe contingency contract to discipline extremely serious behavior problems, they should consult an expert in contingency management.

Urine Screening as a Control

The only way to ascertain drug use in teenagers other than seeing them use drugs is by urinalysis. Parents usually use this testing as a form of control when their adolescent is in the advanced stages of drug use. *Any* drug, including marijuana, can be detected. Many people such as professional athletes and railroad employees are now being asked to submit to this test. A debate has been raging in the media concerning the fallibility of urine screening and the right of employers to require the test as a criteria for continued employment.

This debate should not concern you if your child is in an advanced stage of drug use, although you, of course, want assurance that the test is accurate. Your child's "rights" are not the issue; his or her drug use is. Reportedly, drug-testing kits are now available in drug stores for about $25 which offer testing for marijuana, cocaine, PCP, barbituates or Valium. Test results are purportedly mailed back ten days later. Some experts feel that for various technical reasons, it is inadvisable to use a do-it-yourself mail-order procedure unless there is no reasonable alternative available. There are programs in most metropolitan areas that screen urine when a definite problem is identified. A "problem" is defined when health, academic, psychological or legal problems surface.

6. Counseling, Treatment and Aftercare

DENIAL

Parental Denial

Unfortunately, it's rather common for parents to deny that their child is experimentally, socially or otherwise involved in the local teen alcohol and drug scene — or, perhaps, that such a scene even exists in the community. The teenager tells them, "No, of course I'm not a part of that!" The parents, who desperately *want* to believe this is true, say, "Okay. Good!" Then they close their eyes to the issue. They readily accept their teenager's often flimsy explanations of suspicious incidents and/or behavior. When another parent calls them to discuss specific concerns about the teenagers' activities they say, "Oh, no. You're wrong. Janie said she went to the movies with Charlie that night." If confronted with blatant and irrefutable evidence of their teenager's involvement, they are quick to rationalize it.

Why? Do they just not care? Perhaps, but not necessarily. They may, for example, lack self-confidence and/or have no idea how to deal with the issue. Or they may feel that if they admit to a problem, the entire community will know about it and judge them. There are many reasons for parental denial — the "not-my-kid" syndrome. Yet, whatever the reason, the resulting posture is the same: parents bury their heads in the sand to avoid confronting the issue. Sadly, too many parents continue to dismiss the obvious signs until a telephone call from the hospital emergency room, the police station or the dean's office at school forces them to intervene. When and if it progresses to this point, the parent and the teenager may be facing a very serious problem.

Teenage Denial

It isn't totally surprising that teenagers, when confronted with the fact that they have or are developing a problem with alcohol and/or other drugs, will often deny it vigorously. They don't *want* to have a problem. They want to continue to have fun with their friends, and they want to hold on to their one dependable means of "feeling good" whenever they are down. They refuse to admit that very often it is their drug use that sends them down. At this point, most of the negative health consequences, which usually take some time to develop, seem nebulous to a young person. Likewise, teenagers consider themselves personally — and miraculously — immune to any other consequences of drug use, particularly any serious danger to their lives. Consciously or subconsciously, they also feel supremely confident of their ability to "con" their way out of any trouble with the law or the school administration in the same way they have been conning their parents.

Teen abusers rationalize that some of their friends drink (or smoke, or snort) more than they themselves do, and nobody's calling their friend an abuser or an alcoholic or a drug addict. They feel that if they really couldn't handle it, they could and would quit — no problem. The drug abuser often has a distorted understanding of his own situation and may fail to recognize his own rationalizations. Therefore, a parent can't put much credence in the teenager's assessment of his or her problem situation. Teenage (and adult) drug abusers must hit an unbearably painful bottom point before they will admit they are out of control and willingly seek or accept help. The parents' role is to speed up this bottoming-out process, either alone or with some type of assistance. Only then is there the possibility that the teenager will confront his or her problem and, hopefully, attempt to resolve it.

—— THE DECISION TO GET HELP —— A DIFFICULT ONE!

Don't face it alone — ask for help. This is the most important and usually the most difficult step a distraught parent can take! If you don't know whether you should ask for help, ask yourself, "Is my teenager consistently out of (my) control, totally beyond parental authority and intervention?" Don't hesitate to ask friends, relatives, teachers, school counselors, family doctors, or anyone else who might have some influence to offer needed insight and constructive ideas. They care, and they will want to help *if* they can. Outside help, though, should supplement the family effort, not replace it.

Dr. Bill Porter, Coordinator of Pupil Services/Mental Health Services in Colorado's Cherry Creek School District, suggests that a parent who has a concern about drug or alcohol use contact one of the following people at his child's school: the principal, a counselor, a mental health professional (e.g., psychologist, social worker) or the school nurse. Dr. Porter stresses that parents should select the person with whom they are most comfortable in discussing such a sensitive subject — the one with whom the parent has the most positive relationship. All of these people are knowledgeable resources within the school and would be able to lend assistance. If they do not have the necessary information, they will find the best available resource for the parent.

Some parents feel that the drug related situation is either too complex or involves issues which require professional specialty assistance. Available treatment options are discussed under a separate topic later in this section. However, a misdiagnosis can be made at either extreme. Don't hesitate to be persistent if *you* feel your child has a problem, even though you are told by someone else that he or she is "perfectly normal." Parents, in general, have a notorious reputation for rationalizing troubling changes in their child and denying the possibility of drug involvement, but some professionals (and non-professionals) are also guilty of this. It is frustrating when the parent recognizes a drug problem, goes for much needed help and then can't convince the "expert" there is a problem. Remember, you probably know your child better than anyone. Hang in there until you get satisfaction.

Remember, too, many chemically dependent children are expert con artists and accomplished liars. Some are so adept they can sometimes fool the experts. Once a diagnosis of drug abuse is made or confirmed, the master con artist will try to convince his or her parents that the diagnostician is "overreacting." Don't fall for it! No matter how badly you wish it were true.

WHEN THE SITUATION IS OUT OF CONTROL*

First, let's define what we mean by "out of control." Basically, we're talking about a state of affairs that is beyond our everyday knowledge, as parents, to deal with. Some examples.

- Your teenager has an out-of-control drug experience which leads you to believe there might be a serious problem. For example:

    Public drunkenness in a dangerous way.

    A bad trip from a hallucinogen.

    Reality-distortion or bizarre behavior due to a bad reaction to any drug injected.

- Your teenager has developed an addictive or psychologically dependent usage of a drug, and you find out.

- You find out from the police that your teenager has been arrested for selling drugs or buying drugs.

- Your teenager gets reprimanded or suspended from school or some public place for illegal drug use.

- A suicide attempt or gesture that is drug related is made by your teenager.

Second, if you encounter a crisis, you need to handle it before figuring out what to do or say in order to remedy the problem. Several guidelines are relevant.

- For bad drug reactions or suicide attempts get the person to the hospital emergency room as quickly as possible. (Remember that the drug alcohol can also be taken in toxic quantities.) Take him or her yourself, if feasible, or call 911 and get the ambulance immediately. If possible, find out:

    What drug was taken and how?

    How much was taken over what period of time?

---

*Excerpt with permission from CAP Task Force, Kenneth H. Ash, M.D. and Armon Johannsen, Fort Collins, Colorado.

How long ago was it taken?

Check vital signs.

- If your youngster has been arrested you will be called to the police station, might have to post bail, and will be asked to agree to supervise your teenager's behavior until a hearing. Save your emotional reactions, if you can, until you have time to talk and think them over.

- Talk your reactions over with a friend or spouse — someone you trust. This will help you decide what you want to say and do. Take a day or two before talking with your youngster; you'll be more in control of yourself and consequently more helpful.

Intervening: After you've figured out how you feel and what you plan to do, plan a private, uninterrupted time to talk with your youngster.

Several guidelines are helpful.

- Say it in as calm a manner as possible — have someone there you trust if you're afraid of losing emotional control.

- Say how you felt — scared, embarrassed, angry — but most of all emphasize your concern about what has happened to him.

- Say that something must be done: "I see what happened as an indicator that you, that we *as a family*, have a serious problem — and this is what I propose to do."

- Explain the arrangements you've made: "I've arranged for us to go as a family and talk with _____ to see best how to help."

- Listen to your teenager's reactions but don't postpone going for help.

- Go for help alone if your teenager refuses to go. Then you can find out what to do next.

- When you have made a decision to place your teenager in a treatment center, an intervention specialist can come to your home to guide and support you through this difficult procedure. The therapist can help you state your concerns, present it with love and communicate to the teenager, "I can no longer see you do this to yourself."

What If Your Chemically Dependent Teenager Refuses Treatment?

It may be that after all is said and done, your drug-dependent son or daughter will give you a surly look and tell you, "There's absolutely no way I'm going to any treatment center." In that case you may want to force the teenager to enter treatment. In most states, parents can legally commit their teenage drug abusers to a treatment program, although each state differs somewhat in the particulars. If this is the course you intend to pursue, you might consider consulting an attorney, as well as a treatment facility representative.

Another approach — if your teenager is of suitable age for emancipation — is to inform him or her (in no uncertain terms) that, in your opinion, as long as children are financially dependent on their parents for support, the parents have the right to make such a decision on behalf of the child. If the teenager still refuses to grant you that right, then his or her alternative is to become self-supporting immediately. Being self-supporting means he is totally on his own financially: he must get a job, find a place to live, pay for it and for all other necessities. The teenager should understand that he (or she) is making the decision to leave because he will not accept family rules (e.g., see an alcohol/drug therapist, enter inpatient treatment, etc.). Let him know that when he is ready to accept the rules, he will be welcomed home. If you choose this route, you may want to consult an attorney regarding your continuing legal liability for your minor son's or daughter's actions. However, *before* you choose it, you should consult a qualified mental health professional.

A less controversial method often used before one resorts to more drastic measures is a stringent contingency contract. The consequences for continued drug use or for refusal of counselling or inpatient treatment are extremely severe, but very meaningful to the teenager. For example, you might contract to withdraw all financial assistance for college/trade school. As mentioned previously, a counselor trained in contingency management should help you draw up and present a contract of this magnitude. If the teenager rejects such a contract, this may tell you something.

All these options sound rather harsh; it can be quite painful for you to have to treat your own child in this manner. But consider the alternatives: family disruption and emotional problems; the risk of legal problems; addiction and possible death.

You are the person who must make the final decision regarding what is best for *your* chemically dependent teenager. Hopefully you will involve a mental health professional in the decision. In addition, you might ponder an article by Donald Ian Macdonald, M.D. and Miller Newton, Ph.D., which appears in *Advances in Pediatrics,* entitled "The Clinical Syndrome of Adolescent Drug Abuse" which discusses the problems in turning around the chemically dependent teenager without some type of inpatient treatment. "In his usual environment the chemically dependent teenager is constantly exposed to 'do drug' messages and drug-using 'friends' and has easy access to a wide variety of drugs. He has little willpower and no real interest in quitting. A few children with strong support may be able to quit, but for most, treatment demands complete removal from the environment to either a residential or strict foster care facility. Herculean efforts at supervision by dedicated parents have had some reported success, but for the advanced stages these efforts are unlikely to succeed."

—— TYPES OF AVAILABLE TREATMENT ——

Once parents have made a decision to get professional help for their substance-using teenager, the question becomes, "what kind of help is most appropriate?" Most parents feel not only unqualified to make this determination, but they may also feel so "burned out" with anxiety and frustration that they are tempted to bypass the logical decision-making process. They may flounder around looking desperately for something — just anything — which offers some shred of hope. Adds Tom Brewster, Associate Director of the Addiction Research and Treatment Service (ARTS) at the University of Colorado Health Sciences Center, "The parent is vulnerable to advertising, scare tactics, sensationalism, their own fear of being inadequate, their own guilt, anger, ignorance. They are victims right from the very beginning when they go to seek treatment." The parents can avoid becoming a victim by making a concentrated effort to discover which type of treatment best meets their teenager's needs and carefully scrutinizing all available choices within that treatment category.

There are three types of drug abuse treatments available: general psychiatric psychotherapy or psychological counselling, which is aimed at underlying problems rather than at the "symptom" of drug or alcohol problems; outpatient drug abuse counselling which focuses on drug or alcohol use as the problem, rather than as the symptom of some underlying problem; and inpatient (residential) treatment programs. Some of the inpatient programs treat the alcohol and/or drug use as the problem while others view it as a symptom of underlying problems. Tom Brewster suggests that both the substance *and* adolescence are issues which need to be looked at. To isolate one or the other is a major mistake, he feels. Within each of these treatment categories, there are a myriad of other factors which contribute to the success or failure of such treatment. How can parents sort through all of this and come up with what is best for their child?

The first step is to seek assistance from someone whom you trust and whose opinion you value. Perhaps a knowledgeable school counselor or your physician. This person should be able to refer you directly or indirectly to someone in the mental health field (psychiatrist, social worker, psychiatric nurse, psychologist, *certified* substance abuse counselor) *with training in substance abuse and adolescents,* who can assess your child's problem and recommend a course of action. A well qualified practitioner will most likely be able to refer you to the appropriate type of treatment.

If you have no personal assistance readily available, then you must refer yourself. Sources are listed in the Yellow Pages of the telephone directory under "Alcoholism" and "Drug Addiction." Psychological, psychiatric and social work associations as well as medical schools often have listings. Try your state's drug abuse agency or your church. Call the toll-free numbers listed in Appendix K of this book, or look for a local hotline in your own community. Then, call each practitioner and/or treatment facility on the list you have compiled. Interview them about what they have available. Don't feel intimidated. Ask questions about staff and program credentials as well as their experience and training in adolescent substance abuse disorders.

Many inpatient treatment programs offer evaluations free of charge. A qualified and reliable adolescent treatment program may be helpful in directing you to the appropriate type of treatment. However, be aware that the substance abuse treatment industry in this country is a multi-million dollar industry which does not yet have as refined a standard of conduct and ethics as one finds in the mental health field. It is characterized by an array of qualified and unqualified people. For example, a person whose *only* qualification is that he or she is a recovering alcoholic or drug addict is not a professional, although many excellent professionals are themselves recovering from the disease. Recovering persons who are in the treatment business need to have other training in evaluation and assessment skills. Or they need to be working with a professional who can offer that service.

As a concerned consumer with a great deal at stake — your child — you want to also assure yourself that the "free evaluation" isn't made available for the purpose of "drumming up business." What percentage of these free evaluations result in a referral to the "evaluating" inpatient treatment facility? If you have the impression you are getting a sales pitch, your child is being railroaded or you are being pressured into making a snap decision, you may want to get a second opinion. A good therapist should make recommendations, have no reservations about referring you elsewhere and stress that it is the family's responsibility to make the decision.

Tom Brewster, Associate Director of ARTS, which offers inpatient and outpatient care at both adolescent and adult levels, advocates the least restraining treatment possible. The adolescent should be treated as an outpatient before being treated as an inpatient unless there are extraordinary circumstances: for instance, the child's life is at stake (e.g., convulsive or physically ill with seizures due to substance abuse); he or she is out of control (e.g., chemically dependent, suicidal, psychotic, depressed); the teenager cannot function at home at all for whatever reason (e.g., sexual or physical abuse, a dying parent). An outpatient program might reasonably begin with once or twice-a-week sessions. If the outpatient therapy doesn't yield positive results after a few weeks or months, then it is appropriate to progress into more intensive treatment. This time limitation should depend on the severity of the teenager's problems.

"Positive results" must be measured in the same context. Carefully monitor school and family performance. Test urine regularly or randomly to detect continued drug use. If drug or alcohol problems continue, treatment should be stepped up. This might mean that the child should see the therapist more frequently. It could mean entry into a structured outpatient treatment program which includes not only individual therapy sessions, but also small group sessions and required attendance at a specified number of AA or NA meetings. Eventually, it could mean a day treatment program or inpatient treatment. The hospital-based treatment programs usually last about six weeks. Others may last anywhere from three weeks to a year or more. However, the majority of children who don't meet the criteria for inpatient treatment as outlined above can be helped by outpatient drug abuse treatment. Your child, of course, could be one of the unaccountable exceptions who fails to respond to outpatient care.

In both outpatient and inpatient treatment of adolescent substance disorders, family involvement is critical. A good family therapist can help the family take the necessary action to stop, modify and change the child's behavior. Without the family's active participation, the child is much less likely to respond to treatment. Family members themselves also need help in changing their own reactionary behaviors which have developed as a result of the problem. There are exceptions, however. For example, if the teenager refuses to communicate with the parents, yet expresses a willingness to see a therapist, he or she should be allowed to see a therapist on his own. In such a case, the therapist can communicate with the family separately.

If your child is chemically dependent or has other characteristics which make him or her a candidate for an inpatient treatment program, you should investigate the program thoroughly before entrusting your child to the facility. The following are some questions not previously mentioned which you should consider:

- ✔ **What are the specific goals of the program?** — The issue of adolescence should be involved as well as a good family and aftercare program. Another very important goal is the child's reintegration with his or her family.

- ✔ **Is the program structured or unstructured?** — A good program should be clearly structured. How long is it? What will the child's day be like? Is there group and/or individual therapy? How often? What is required of patients? Does the structure include substantial parental involvement? If parents are restricted, they need to ask why.

- ✔ **Is the program drug free?** — If there isn't random urine monitoring or 24 hour supervision, you should be skeptical. How tolerant is the program of continued drug use? If there is more than minimal tolerance, be skeptical. Do they stress detoxification? Reportedly, adolescents rarely need detox.

- ✔ **What is the program's attitude about specific drugs?** — Does the program consider alcohol and marijuana as "less serious" than other drugs? This could be a dangerous viewpoint. Does the program treat only a particular drug? Usually if you stop a kid from using one, they will use another.

- ✔ **Are adolescents treated separately from adults?** — This is an important issue. First of all, adolescents have some unique problems. Secondly, adolescent girls are especially vulnerable to sexual abuse from hard core adult males who will take advantage of them. Thirdly, kids of either sex do not need sick adults as role models.

- ✔ **How does the program define "successful" treatment?** — This is a loaded question, because success depends on how dysfunctional a child was when entering treatment. The program's success in treating a particular child can be determined only after a minimum of one year follow-up. Distrust purportedly high success rates which lack scientific back-up.

Finally, ask about the cost of various treatment options. The cost of outpatient care may range from zero in a public clinic to $120 per hour in a private psychiatric practice. More intensive treatment could range from $150 per day for a day care program to $300 and up per day in a private hospital-based inpatient program. Several questions might be asked. How much does it cost? Is it publicly or privately funded or a combination of both? Are charges based on income? Does the treatment qualify for health insurance coverage? If you carry health insurance, call the company and check your coverage. Describe the type of treatment and certification. If it is covered, ask about the deductible, the percent or specific amount of coverage and the limitations or restrictions. Also check the reimbursement procedure.

After completing this exhaustive investigation, you are ready to make a decision. Once you select a treatment option, set aside your doubts and go for it. Commit whatever time, effort and family modification is necessary to make this inpatient or outpatient treatment work for your child.

THE PROBLEM OF AFTERCARE

What Is Aftercare?

Aftercare is the continued nurturing of a teenager after he has been eased from a structured treatment program. During the period of inpatient treatment, the teenager is completely removed from the usual environment and somewhat isolated from certain friends and family. In this restricted and controlled environment, the adolescent is forced to abstain from drug use of any kind.

The teenager gradually becomes an integral part of a group consisting of other teens with alcohol/drug problems who are also in treatment. Individually and as a group, the teenagers support each other as they are guided by professional staff members through the initial physical, mental, and emotional recovery process. Thus, the treatment center, set apart from the outside world, becomes a safe, supportive, healing womb to troubled teenagers as they learn to deal with problems and frustrations without the use of chemical substances. "Going home" breaks the umbilical cord.

Why Is It Necessary?

When the teenagers return to their normal environment (home, school, etc.) they are once again available for exposure to "do drug" messages, drug using "friends" and easy access to all kinds of drugs. Some of their peers, perhaps, even their parents and teachers, may think that the drug problem is all taken care of and that's the end of it. Some of their "druggie" friends may think now that they are "out of jail"(treatment) they are anxious to get back into the swing of the drug scene. Neither extreme is at all supportive to the recovering teenager's continued sobriety and/or freedom from drugs.

One of the major problems in teenagers' continued recovery is that people (including the teenagers themselves) often expect too much too soon. In actuality, the recovering teen needs constant reinforcement of the new techniques and skills learned during treatment. It is also important that these young people have a sense of belonging to a group that offers a positive influence. They cannot afford to be around their old "druggie" friends. Yet, it isn't easy to find friends who can understand where they're coming from and be supportive.

Although some of their "straight" friends may be extremely supportive, many of them may have been alienated at some point by the teenager's drug use and may be skeptical about renewing or continuing the old friendship. Finding out who "real" friends are can be a painful experience for the recovering teenager. In addition, some parents may be unwilling to let their children associate with a former drug user. Recovering teens are faced with the problem of not only finding new friends, but also new places to go and things to do. Their old stomping grounds and activities are probably off limits because they are related to old drug habits. He or she should not have to face these problems alone.

What Is Needed?

The key to continuing recovery is *maintaining* the personal and relationship changes after the teenagers are off the drug(s). They need to have a program or plan with reinforcements and check points built in and realize the plan has to be long term. One of the most effective tools for reinforcement is a peer support group made up of recovering teenagers.

The need also exists for parent support groups. Not only is knowledgeable and positive parental involvement critical for the teenager's continued recovery, but the parents are also in a stage of recovery and need this outside support. The pressure of a chemically dependent teenager in the family is very often destructive to family structure and relationships. Thus, alcoholism/drug addiction is often called the "family disease."

What Type Of Aftercare Is Available?

Most treatment centers provide some type of outpatient aftercare program for the teenager who is leaving the center after a period of intense therapy. These aftercare programs can last anywhere from six weeks to several months. There are undoubtedly as many available aftercare options as there are inpatient treatment options. However, an investigation of several reputable short-term treatment facilities in the Metro-Denver area uncovered several common denominators in the aftercare approach. Reportedly, these common features are customary in many other treatment programs around the country.

Shortly before the patient is released, counselors meet with the recovering teenager and his or her parents to develop a "Home Aftercare Contract" tailored to the particular situation. It includes the following: 1) Attend one aftercare meeting at the center weekly. Attend three Alcoholics Anonymous (AA) and/or Narcotics Anonymous (NA) meetings per week. 2) Find a sponsor (big brother or sister) who has had at least one year of sobriety and will be readily available for one-on-one-support. With the sponsor's guidance, continue to read and study the AA "big book," the AA "24 hour book" plus notes and handouts from the sessions.

Following the contracted aftercare period, the student is encouraged to voluntarily return to treatment center meetings, as well as AA or NA meetings. A directory of time and location of local AA, NA and Al-Anon meetings is available to anyone. Call the number listed in your local telephone book for those organizations. If there is no listing, contact the national offices (listed in Appendix K) for information about groups meeting in nearby communities.

The School's Role in Aftercare

School aftercare programs, if available, also differ. The following example offers insight into a "before and after" situation. In the spring of 1985, 18 year-old Brian, a recovering high school student, shared his frustrating "re-entry" experience. He described the school's "Re-entry Staffing," a meeting which he was required to attend before returning to classes. Among those present were his mother, a widow, as well as his guidance counselor, the head of the counselling department, an assistant principal, a dean and the school psychologist. The group discussed the treatment program and the problems Brian would encounter at school. He said many staff members emphasized their availability and willingness to support him in any way he needed. They also suggested that he continue to see the school psychologist regularly, as well as participate in the regular weekly discussion sessions for students with problems of various types. Brian said he attended only one of these general sessions and felt it was not helpful.

He felt strongly that students returning from drug treatment centers are part of a unique fraternity which only those who have been there can understand. Both he and his student sponsor, another recovering senior, discussed with the school principal the need for a school-based support program, which would address individual problems in maintaining sobriety within the local school and social environment. At that time, the principal felt a separate support group for recovering students was inappropriate for school sponsorship. Brian and his friend Tim were also unsuccessful in trying to form a teenage support group in the community. Although the community alcohol/drug task force and several members of AA lent their support and assistance, it proved impossible to get the recovering kids from his high school together outside the school environment. Primarily this was due to lack of motivation and scheduling problems created by after-school jobs and widely diverse activities. Many of the boys' recovering school mates either dropped out of school or returned to the drug culture.

The principal, however subsequently reversed his position. In January 1986, a school-based re-entry support group was formed. The group, which is facilitated by concerned and dedicated staff members, meets daily for one class period. Although membership in the group is optional, regular attendance is expected after a commitment has been made. Three of the weekly meetings are facilitating sessions; two are for speakers or other related activities. Upon entry into the group, the recovering teenager is asked for a commitment to try and remain substance-free. If a student "slips," he or she is asked to share the experience with the other members of the group and enlist their support in his or her effort to "try again."

Apparently, the group has become somewhat of the "in" thing for youngsters returning to school from treatment, and a high percentage are choosing to participate. Prior to January 1986, there was a substantial dropout rate among students returning from treatment programs. It would appear that more students are now staying in school. A study comparing students who have elected to participate in the support group to those who have not shows that the students who have chosen to be involved have better school attendance, better grades, fewer dropouts and fewer reports of negative interaction with the deans. There is no urine testing involved in the support program, so actual drug use or non-use cannot be monitored. However, other factors indicate that many of these students may be remaining drug-free.

The success of this effort has motivated the staff to consider focusing on other related issues. Members of the task force hope they will consider making available a regular AA meeting before, during or after school, which would be open to *any* student having an alcohol or drug problem. Perhaps another undertaking at some point could be sponsorship of an evening parent support group and an Alateen meeting for students whose parents have drug problems. Opportunities abound for schools to be positively involved in assisting recovering students, their parents and the children of drug-dependent parents.

——— LOCAL SOURCES OF HELP ———

Agency/Individual	Telephone Number

7. For Kids Only

──── A PERSONAL CHECKLIST FOR ──── ADOLESCENTS*

1. Does it bother you if someone says that maybe you're drinking too much?

2. Have you ever missed school or work because of drinking or drugs?

3. Do you drink to build up your confidence, to feel more relaxed around other people?

4. Do you drink or use drugs by yourself?

5. Do you hang out with a crowd that drinks or uses drugs?

6. Do your friends drink LESS than you?

7. Do you use alcohol to escape from home, study or worries about your friends?

8. Have you borrowed money or gotten into financial trouble to buy drugs?

9. Have you lost or changed friends because of alcohol or drugs?

10. Do you drink until the bottle or six-pack is empty?

11. Are you turned off by lectures on drugs?

12. Have you ever gotten a ticket for driving while using drugs? Been in trouble with the police?

13. Have you ever had memory lapses while drinking?

14. Do you feel guilty about your use of drugs?

―――――――――
*Source pamphlets for portions of this section made available by the National Institute on Drug Abuse

15. Do you hide your drug use or drinking from others?

16. Do you drink or use drugs to relax when you feel tense or nervous? Do you feel more powerful?

17. Do you ever drink to get high before going out on a date?

18. Have you been in trouble outside your home because of drinking or drugs?

19. Do you sometimes get drunk or stoned when you didn't intend to?

20. Do you sometimes gulp down a drink rather than drink it slowly?

21. Have you ever had a drink, joint or pill in the morning?

22. Have you ever been hospitalized because of alcohol or drugs?

23. Have your grades or work suffered because of using alcohol or drugs?

24. Have you ever stolen money to buy alcohol or drugs?

25. Do many of your activities revolve around drinking?

26. Is drinking affecting your reputation?

27. Do you think you have a problem with alcohol or drugs?

28. Have you ever been in an accident while drinking or using drugs?

One yes indicates a danger, two a high probability, three a problem.

When A Friend Has A Problem With Drugs

When you're very young, most of your ideas of what to do come from your parents. As you grow older, the ideas of your friends begin to take on more and more importance. They become the ones you ask for advice and help. This is a natural part of growing up. And it works both ways: *you* are probably the biggest influence on your friends' lives.

Suppose a friend got involved with drugs. What would you do? Maybe nothing at all. "It's his business. This is a free country isn't it?" That's one point of view. But if you are really a friend, it is your business. You've heard of "peer pressure." You're it.

Drug abuse is often a symptom of another problem. People use drugs to change the way they feel and get away from their problems. Good friends help one another through difficult times.

Help your friend figure out why he or she is hurt, angry or upset.

If your friend's drug problem is beyond your ability to help, if it frightens you, or it's an emergency, call one of the agencies in Appendix K, or talk to your parents.

When Your Friend's Parent Has a Problem With Drugs and/or Alcohol

You may be aware that your friend's mom or dad has a drug or alcohol problem because you have heard adults talk about it, or perhaps you have seen evidence of it first-hand. Your friend — let's call her Sue — may even have told you about it. On the other hand, she may not have said a word and get very prickly and defensive if you try to bring it up. Even though you are one of her closest and most trusted friends, the problem may be too painful or embarrassing for her to discuss. How would you feel if your mom, for example, were a "druggie" or a heavy boozer? Regardless of how it seems at times, Sue values your loyal friendship much more that you can possibly realize. It lessens the pain of loneliness and depression caused by her mother's drug dependency. In addition, her dad may have his hands full with Mom and not be able to give Sue the support she so desperately needs.

Sue has a lot of disturbing feelings other than embarrassment and loneliness. You may feel hurt and confused at times, thinking they are directed at you, when really they are aimed at her problem mom. Hang in there! Try to understand and encourage her to share them. She desperately needs someone to just listen, but may be reluctant to ask. At first you may be overwhelmed.

Sue feels angry that her mother is doing this to her, yet she still loves her and wants to protect and take care of her. She feels guilty that she can't solve the problem, and may even feel that she is the cause of the problem. She may have other worries as well. She may be afraid that sometime while her mom is blasted she will accidentally harm herself, burn down the house or have an automobile accident. She is afraid that her friends will ridicule her because of her mom's behavior. She may even be afraid of physical abuse. Probably she is feeling anger and resentment about the verbal abuse and added household/babysitting responsibilities she puts up with when mom's smashed or buzzed. Overall, Sue feels very badly about her mother and not very good about herself.

These are tough feelings for a kid to handle. Her mom's behavior may be telling her that "drugs are okay," but just don't use them like Mom does. Sue could be tempted to use drugs herself to escape her bad feelings for a little while. If this happens, try to make her realize that "drugs are *not* okay." Unless Sue is adopted, she has another important reason to avoid even experimenting with drugs or alcohol. Drug addiction and alcoholism tend to run in family lines, so she may have an inherited physical susceptibility to the disease of addiction. If she tries drugs, she may eventually end up just like her mom — a very sick person.

What can you do besides listen and try to convince her not to use drugs as a cop-out? Because Sue's family life may be a real mess, you might ask if Sue could be included in some of your family's activities. Sue also needs someone to help her deal with her feelings about her mother's problem. You, of course, aren't trained to do this. Encourage her to share the situation with her school counselor. The counselor will not only sympathize, understand, and offer advice, but he or she can also suggest some places where Sue can go to get help, like the school psychologist or Alateen. Talk this over with your parents. They will probably want to help just as you do. But remember, you can't hold yourself responsible for solving Sue's problem for her. If things don't work out, don't lay a guilt trip on yourself. You have done the best you can, and that's all that can be expected of you.

Handling Peer Pressure And Drugs

Here are some ways to say "no" to drugs. Remember, you have the right to!

- Give a reason. If you know the facts, someone telling you that it feels good to be stoned won't fool you. You can say, "No, I know it's bad for me. I feel fine right now." You might add, "I think you're a wimp to mess with that stuff."
- Have something else to do. "No thanks. I'm going to get something to eat."
- Be prepared for different kinds of pressure. There are different levels of peer pressure. It can start out friendly or teasing; if so, you can respond the same way. If the pressure seems threatening, then you might just have to walk away.
- Make it simple. Just say "No." You don't have to explain why you don't want to use marijuana if you don't want to. You can just say, "No thanks." If that doesn't work, you can always say, "No thanks again" or even stronger, "No way. Read my lips."

- Avoid the situation. If you see or know of places where people often use drugs, stay away from those places. If you hear that people will be using drugs at a party, don't go.

PRECAUTIONS SUGGESTED BY LAW ENFORCEMENT OFFICERS

In Public Places

- Anytime you go any place where people gather, you should not go alone.

- Avoid unruly crowds.

- Report any suspicious person or someone who approaches you with anything illegal to the nearest store employee or security officer.

- If you have to go to any area which is relatively isolated, always have someone accompany you. This is true for bathrooms, elevators, stairways, and dressing rooms.

In Parking Areas

- When you park your car somewhere, perhaps to pile in with friends, always lock it.

- When they drop you off ask them to wait. Don't walk to your car if someone is standing nearby.

- Always look in the back seat before you get in.

When Walking Home

- Don't walk outside your neighborhood alone — particularly in the evening. Don't ever walk or bicycle while intoxicated. Call someone to pick you up or stay put. WHY? A 15-year-old Colorado youth passed out a few blocks from his house while walking home from a nearby party. His body was discovered the next morning. An autopsy showed death was due to toxic alcohol overdose. However, authorities speculated that he would have died from exposure anyway as the result of lying unconscious in the snow overnight.

- Even when accompanied by another person do the following:

    Call home before you leave and let them know what time to

expect you and exactly what route you are taking.

If no one is home leave the same information at your departure point and call them immediately upon arriving home.

If a strange or suspicious car or person approaches you, be ready to run. Go to the nearest possible place for help.

When Friends You Are With Are Doing Something Illegal

- Be aware of vandalism, shoplifting, illegal possession, etc.
- Do *not* become involved. Walk away immediately and then report the incident to a responsible adult.
- Be aware of how your involvement might be interpreted under the law. For example, even if you don't steal anything, your standing watch while a friend shoplifts could make you an accessory to a crime. If you help plan some vandalism and/or suggest a location where the vandalism takes place (e.g., the home of someone you don't like), you might be charged with criminal conspiracy, even though you don't actually participate in the vandalism.

When Confronted With A Fight Or Other Altercation

- Do not become *directly* involved. Not only could you get hurt, particularly if a weapon suddenly appears, but you could also be charged with assault or fighting.
- Be an accurate witness.

When an Officer Is Called to the Scene (e.g., a "Beer Bust")

- Wait until the situation is under control and follow officers' instructions.
- If you were a witness to the incident, inform the officer(s) (either at the scene or by telephone at a more appropriate time).

NOTE: Look in Appendix G of this booklet under "Other Potential Crimes Chargeable" to see what type of behavior you should avoid in this situation and why.

You and the Law

Most teenagers are very vocal about demanding their "rights" as citizens and young adults. Yet, when it comes to accepting their citizen responsibilities and legal liabilities, some of these teenagers consistently cop-out with, "Oh, the cops can't/won't do anything. I'm just a kid."

Don't count on it, particularly if you live in a larger community. Instead of getting a slap on the wrist or a "lecture and release," you might be charged and taken into custody — even for a petty offense. If you're under a certain age, usually 18, you'll probably be diverted into the juvenile system, and if the crime is very minor, you may suffer relatively light consequences.

However, even if you eventually "get off," the entire procedure isn't a real fun experience. Imagine yourself being frisked, handcuffed and shoved into the back of a squad car for a trip to headquarters, where you will be put into a holding cell until your parents can come to pick you up. What if they're out of town? Consider the inconvenience of the subsequent court appearance(s) and the expense of hiring an attorney and/or paying fines and court costs. Finally, think about how a police record might affect your future. You'd be surprised at the background information required on job and college applications.

On the other hand, you may get the book thrown at you, or, in some cases, be charged as an adult. The legal process is very discretionary. Whether you find yourself facing a minor petty offense, a misdemeanor or a more serious felony is largely determined by the decision of the arresting officer and/or the prosecuting attorney. The penalties, if you are found guilty, are determined by the presiding judge. Thus, anytime you break the law —any law — you are playing Russian roulette with your future, and the odds may be heavily stacked against you.

Ignorance of the law is not a valid defense. It's your responsibility to be aware of the laws in your local jurisdiction, as well as federal and state laws. You might begin by finding out if there are teen curfew restrictions in your area. Call your local police department. They are very willing to provide the information, and you needn't give your name. You should also be aware of the penalties for committing various illegal, or criminal, acts before you consider giving in to peer pressure. For example, take a look below at the potential penalties facing a teenager in Aurora, Colorado who chooses to mess around with alcohol and/or other drugs.

Alcohol — Seventeen with a tall Coors in your hand? Under the Colorado Liquor and Beer Code, the maximum penalty for a seventeen-year-old under these circumstances is a $500 to $5,000 fine and/or 90 days in a detention facility. Realistically, a penalty of this magnitude would probable not be invoked, but it is within the realm of possibility. Suppose the district attorney decides to crack down hard as an example to others — and *you* are the example.

Marijuana — Have a couple of joints stashed in the glove compartment? Be prepared for a fine up to $100 on a first offense. If you have more than one ounce or if you sell any, you face felony charges.

Cocaine — You've got to be kidding! Possession of *any* amount of cocaine is a felony any way you look at it. You could be facing up to two years in a detention facility and a *very* hefty fine. *Selling* any illegal drug is also a felony.

Paraphernalia — Carrying around a "roach clip" as a conversation piece? In Colorado, possession of an item which a reasonable person would know is for the purpose of using illicit drugs is a misdemeanor, even if the item has never been used for drugs.

Obtaining and/or using a false ID — Underage and want to pick up a little booze? You may only be charged with giving false information or using a false ID, both misdemeanors. However, felony charges such as forgery or criminal impersonation might also be appropriate.

Quite probably, the laws and penalties in your area differ somewhat, but you get the drift. Look in Appendix G to get a more indepth look at the potential liabilities for a Colorado teenager who gets involved in a keg party. Then check out the applicable penalties if the same party had occurred in your community. The laws you are subject to may be even tougher.

Appendices

A. Controlled Substances: Uses & Effects 144
B. Awareness Test For Parents 146
C. Specific Signs and Symptoms of
   Adolescent Drug Use 145
D. Stages in Adolescent Chemical Use 150
E. How to Give a Successful Teenage Party 151
F. What You Can Expect if Your Child
   is Arrested 153
G. Potential Legal Liabilities of the
   "Kegger Scenario" 154
H. An Open Letter to Parents and Teenage Drivers 158
I. Sample Contingency Contract 161
J. Sample Substance Abuse Policy and Procedure 162
K. Additional Resources and Reading 171

APPENDIX A

CONTROLLED SUBSTANCES:

	Drugs	Trade or Other Names	Medical Uses	Physical Dependence	Psychological Dependence
NARCOTICS	Opium	Dover's Powder, Paregoric, Parepectolin	Analgesic, antidiarrheal	High	High
	Morphine	Morphine, Pectoral Syrup	Analgesic, antitussive		
	Codeine	Codeine, Empirin Compound with Codeine, Robitussin A-C	Analgesic, antitussive	Moderate	Moderate
	Heroin	Diacetylmorphine, Horse, Smack	Under investigation	High	High
	Hydromorphone	Dilaudid	Analgesic		
	Meperidine (Pethidine)	Demerol, Pethadol	Analgesic		
	Methadone	Dolophine, Methadone, Methadose	Analgesic, heroin substitute		
	Other Narcotics	LAAM, Leritine, Levo-Dromoran, Percodan, Tussionex, Fentanyl, Darvon*, Talwin*, Lomotil	Analgesic, antidiarrheal, antitussive	High-Low	High-Low
DEPRESSANTS	Chloral Hydrate	Noctec, Somnos	Hypnotic	Moderate	Moderate
	Barbiturates	Amobarbital, Phenobarbital, Butisol, Phenoxbarbital, Secobarbital, Tuinal	Anesthetic, anticonvulsant, sedative, hypnotic	High-Moderate	High-Moderate
	Glutethimide	Doriden	Sedative, hypnotic	High	High
	Methaqualone	Optimil, Parest, Quaalude, Somnafac, Sopor			
	Benzodiazepines	Ativan, Azene, Clonopin, Dalmane, Diazepam, Librium, Serax, Tranxene, Valium, Verstran	Anti-anxiety, anti-convulsant, sedative, hypnotic	Low	Low
	Other Depressants	Equanil, Miltown, Noludar Placidyl, Valmid	Anti-anxiety, sedative, hypnotic	Moderate	Moderate
STIMULANTS	Cocaine†	Coke, Flake, Snow	Local anesthetic	Possible	High
	Amphetamines	Biphetamine, Delcobese, Desoxyn, Dexedrine, Mediatric	Hyperkinesis, narcolepsy, weight control		
	Phenmetrazine	Preludin			
	Methylphenidate	Ritalin			
	Other Stimulants	Adipex, Bacarate, Cylert, Didrex, Ionamin, Plegine, Pre-Sate, Sanorex, Tenuate, Tepanil, Voranil			
HALLUCINOGENS	LSD	Acid, Microdot	None	None	Degree unknown
	Mescaline and Peyote	Mesc, Buttons, Cactus			
	Amphetamine Variants	2,5-DMA, PMA, STP, MDA, MMDA, TMA, DOM, DOB		Unknown	
	Phencyclidine	PCP, Angel Dust, Hog	Veterinary anesthetic	Degree unknown	High
	Phencyclidine Analogs	PCE, PCPy, TCP	None	None	Degree unknown
	Other Hallucinogens	Bufotenine, Ibogaine, DMT, DET, Psilocybin, Psilocyn			
CANNABIS	Marihuana	Pot, Acapulco Gold, Grass, Reefer, Sinsemilla, Thai Sticks	Under Investigation	Degree unknown	Moderate
	Tetrahydrocannabinol	THC			
	Hashish	Hash	None		
	Hashish Oil	Hash Oil			

NOTE: The chart above does not include dangerous "inhalants." The following information is excerpted from the U.S. Dept. of Education booklet, *Schools Without Drugs: What Works*. Types listed include:

Nitrous Oxide ("laughing gas", "whippets") — propellant for whipped cream in aerosol cans, metal cylinder sold with a balloon or pipe.

Amyl Nitrate ("poppers", "snappers") — clear yellowish liquid in ampules.

Butyl Nitrate ("rush", "bolt", "locker room", "bullet", "climax") — packaged in small bottles.

Chlorohydrocarbons ("aerosol sprays") — aerosol paint cans, cleaning fluid.

Hydrocarbons ("solvents") — cans of aerosol propellants, gasoline, glue, paint thinner.

APPENDIX A | 145

USES & EFFECTS

Tolerance	Duration of Effects (in hours)	Usual Methods of Administration	Possible Effects	Effects of Overdose	Withdrawal Syndrome
Yes	3-6	Oral, smoked	Euphoria, drowsiness, respiratory depression, constricted pupils, nausea	Slow and shallow breathing, clammy skin, convulsions, coma, possible death	Watery eyes, runny nose, yawning, loss of appetite, irritability, tremors, panic, chills and sweating, cramps, nausea
		Oral, injected, smoked			
		Oral, injected			
		Injected, sniffed, smoked			
	12-24	Oral, injected			
	Variable				
Possible	5-8	Oral	Slurred speech, disorientation, drunken behavior without odor of alcohol	Shallow respiration, cold and clammy skin, dilated pupils, weak and rapid pulse, coma, possible death	Anxiety, insomnia, tremors, delirium, convulsions, possible death
Yes	1-16				
	4-8	Oral, injected			
Possible	1-2	Sniffed, injected	Increased alertness, excitation, euphoria, increased pulse rate and blood pressure, insomnia, loss of appetite	Agitation, increase in body temperature, hallucinations, convulsions, possible death	Apathy, long periods of sleep, irritability, depression, disorientation
Yes	2-4	Oral, injected			
		Oral			
Yes	8-12	Oral	Illusions and hallucinations, poor perception of time and distance	Longer, more intense "trip" episodes, psychosis, possible death	Withdrawal syndrome not reported
	Up to days	Oral, injected			
	Variable	Smoked, oral, injected			
Possible		Oral, Injected, smoked, sniffed			
Yes	2-4	Smoked, oral	Euphoria, relaxed inhibitions, increased appetite, disoriented behavior	Fatigue, paranoia, possible psychosis	Insomnia, hyperactivity, and decreased appetite occasionally reported

* Not designated a narcotic under the CSA
† Designated a narcotic under the CSA

AWARENESS TEST FOR PARENTS*

Take this test for each child alone, with your spouse. Then compare your results with your spouse's so that, if possible, you can present a consolidated, unified awareness test to each child. Ask each other how objective, how factual, how unemotional you are in each of your answers.

1. Has your child's personality changed noticeably and are there sudden inappropriate mood changes (irritability, unprovoked hostility or giddiness)?
2. Is he or she less responsible for chores, getting to school on time, household rules?
3. Does your child seem to be losing old friends and hanging out with a drinking or partying group?
4. Is there trouble at school — grades dropping, missing classes or interest waning in school activities?
5. Are you missing money or items that could be converted to cash?
6. Is your liquor supply dwindling — are you sure it's not evaporating or turning into colored water? What about your pills?
7. Do you consistently hear about your child's behavior from friends, neighbors, or teachers?
8. Is your child in trouble with the law?
9. Does your child react belligerently to comments, criticism, or remarks about his or her drinking?
10. Does your child turn off to talks, television shows, or literature about alcoholism or drug abuse?
11. Does your child get into fights with other youngsters?
12. Are there signs of medical or emotional problems (ulcers, gastritis, liver problems, depression, overwhelming anxiety, suicide talk or gestures)?
13. Is he or she irresponsible behind the wheel of an automobile?
14. Is your child generally dishonest?
15. Does your child volunteer to clean up after adult cocktail parties but neglect other household chores?
16. Do you find obvious signs such as a stash of bottles, beer cans or drug paraphernalia in the bedroom, basement or garage?
17. Do you detect physical signs such as alcohol on the breath, pupil change, redness of eyes, slurred speech or staggering?

---

*This document was provided by Saint Luke's Hospital, Adolescent Addictions Recovery Unit, Denver, Co, (303) 869-2550.

18. Does your child spend a lot of time alone behind closed doors in the bedroom, recreation room, or listening to the stereo?
19. Have your child's sleeping and/or eating habits changed?
20. Have your child's relationships with other family members deteriorated? Is he or she withdrawn or uncommunicative?
21. Have your child's dress habits and personal hygiene significantly changed?
22. Has your child experimented with alcohol and/or drugs? What, when, where?
23. How much money has your child spent the last day, week, month on alcohol and other drugs?
24. Would you classify your child as a non-user, a social user, or an abuser of alcohol and drugs?
25. Are your children concerned about your own use of alcohol and other drugs?
26. Is your child concerned about his or her use of alcohol, or other drugs, including marijuana?

If YES is the answer to 5 or more of these questions, then there are strong indications that your child may be in trouble with alcohol, marijuana, or other drugs. Beware, however, of your own prejudices, or your own emotions and attitudes influencing your answers.

- Are you being objective and factual about your child's behavior?
- Do you know your child's friends and their parents?
- When your child goes "out", do you know where he/she goes and what he/she does?
- Do you set a good example by not using alcohol or drugs inappropriately?
- Do you have honest, open, factual, unemotional discussions about alcohol and drugs with your child?
- Do you really understand the problems that your child faces in today's society?

If YES is the answer to these questions, then there are strong indications that your relationship with your child is constructive.

Alcoholism and drug addiction can be successfully treated. A lot depends on you, your attitudes, and your action. If a member of your family or a friend has an alcohol or drug problem. **TAKE ACTION.**

SPECIFIC SIGNS AND SYMPTOMS OF ADOLESCENT DRUG USE

The following list of signs and symptoms was provided by the CAP Task Force, Fort Collins, Colorado. If a number of these signs and symptoms suddenly show up, you might suspect that chemical abuse could be present.

Physical Symptoms

- Change in activity level — periods of lethargy or fatigue (common with marijuana, alcohol, sedatives, cocaine, heroin and pot). Periods of hyperactivity (common with marijuana, alcohol, amphetamines and other stimulants).
- Change in appetite — varying from increase to decrease, and cravings for certain foods (sweets are common with marijuana). Also present is an increase or decrease in weight.
- Incoordination — staggering gait, slow movements, dropping objects, clumsiness, falling.
- Speech patterns — slurred or garbled speech, flat or expressionless speech, pressured speech (fast talking), forgetting thoughts and ideas, incomplete sentences.
- Shortness of breath, hacking cough, peculiar odor to breath and clothes (often with marijuana).
- Red eyes, watery eyes, droop to eyelids.
- Runny nose, increased susceptibility to infections and colds.
- Change in sleeping habits — staying up all night, sleeping all day, insomnia, excess sleeping, refusal to wake up.
- Change in appearance — change in style of clothes, less concern about appearance, sloppy, unkept.
- Severe agitation, lack of concentration, shaking, tremors of extremities, nausea, vomiting, sweats, chills (may be early withdrawal syndrome from drugs).
- Distortion in time — short times may feel much longer, reaction time sluggish.
- "Needle tracks" — long-sleeved shirts in all weather. Tracks may be in hidden areas, such as back of legs.

Social And Emotional Changes

- Mood alteration — changes and "swings" in mood — overly happy, gregariousness to irritability, anxiety, violence, bizarreness, depressed mood, outburst of anger.

- Thought alterations — lack of thought, strange and bizarre thinking, hallucinations, paranoid delusion, suspiciousness, depressed thoughts, suicidal thoughts.
- Withdrawal, secretiveness, deviousness, vagueness, hypersensitivity, placing his room "off-limits" to family.
- Sudden changes in friends, disdain for old friends, new people calling, frequenting new hangouts, people stopping by for very short periods.
- Drop in school performance, truancy, resentment toward teachers, avoiding schoolwork (or not bringing books home), lack of interest and concentration span in school, hobbies, anything ("amotivational syndrome").
- New idols — especially drug-using rock stars, songs with drug lyrics, older kids.
- Legal problems — late hours, traffic violations, assaultiveness, disrespect for police, eventually possession of paraphernalia and drugs.
- Resentment toward all authority.
- Presence of paraphernalia, incense, room deodorizer, eyedrop bottles, seeds and drugs.
- Flagrant disregard for all rules — school, home, legal.

NOTE: Many of these characteristics are typical of the non-drug using adolescent. Parents should look for changes in and exaggeration of behavior as well as combinations of these characteristics.

APPENDIX D

STAGES OF DRUG ABUSE*

STAGE	MOOD ALTERATION	FEELINGS	DRUGS	SOURCES	BEHAVIOR	FREQUENCY
1. Learning the mood swing	Euphoria ↻ Normal Pain	Feel good Few consequences	Tobacco Marijuana Alcohol	"Friends"	Little detectable change Moderate "after the fact" lying	Progresses to weekend usage
2. Seeking the mood swing	Euphoria ↻ Normal Pain	Excitement Early guilt	All of the above plus: Inhalants Hash oil, hashish "Ups" "Downs" Prescriptions	Buying	Drop extracurricular activities and hobbies Mixed friends (straight and druggie) Dress changing Erratic school performance and skipping Unpredictable mood and attitude swings "Conning" behavior	Weekend use progressing to 4-5 times per week Some solo use
3. Preoccupation with the mood swing	Euphoria ↻ Normal Pain	Euphoric highs Double including: Severe shame and guilt Depression Suicidal thoughts	All of the above plus: Mushrooms PCP LSD Cocaine	Selling	"Cool" appearance Straight friends dropped Family fights (verbal and physical) Stealing — police incidents Pathologic lying School failure, skipping, expulsion, jobs lost	Daily Frequent solo use
4. Using drugs to feel normal	Euphoria ↻ Normal Pain	Chronic Guilt Shame Remorse Depression	Whatever is available	Any way possible	Physical deterioration (weight loss, chronic cough) Severe mental deterioration (memory loss and flashbacks) Paranoia, volcanic anger and aggression School drop-out Frequent overdosing	All day every day

*Reproduced with permission from Macdonald, D. I., and Newton, M.: The Clinical Syndrome of Adolescent Drug Abuse, in Barness, L.A., et al. (Eds.), *Advances in Pediatrics*, Volume 28. Copyright © 1981 by Year Book Medical Publishers, Inc., Chicago.

HOW TO GIVE A SUCCESSFUL TEENAGE PARTY*

The planning of a social activity is the most important aspect of the activity, ensuring its success. It provides an opportunity for dialogue and cooperation between parents and teenagers and for the teaching of social skills. The fun and success of your party will be a direct result of your efforts!

Parties are usually more fun and successful if given with others. Parents and other adults will need to be involved, but teens should take responsibility for decisions (with guidance if needed). Teens also need to remember adults are legally responsible for minors.

Initial Planning Between Teenagers

- Set ground rules (e.g. no alcohol or drugs, rules of house, etc.).
- Agree on basic plan for party and work together to make the party a success.

Parent Responsibilities

Be visible, available, and supportive. Keep a low profile. The number of adults depends on size of the party and activities.

Be visible when guests arrive.

Help (like in kitchen) so party givers can enjoy party.

Enforce no drugs or alcohol rule.

Teen Responsibilities

Take responsibility for preparation.
Start activities, let people know where things are.
Encourage guests to participate.
Discourage undesirable behavior
Have fun yourself.

Purpose of Party, What Kind of Party?

Birthday • Costume • Celebration • Class • Theme • Holiday • Beach • Team • Surprise • Bike hike — picnic • Progressive dinner • Etc.

Special Activities To Be Included In Party (Suggestions)

cards • games • band • guitar — singer • backgammon • water games • records • pumpkin carving • dancing • basketball • hayride • haunted house • frisbees • tug o' war • movies • art project • horseshoes • kites • magician • ice cream making • ping pong • pool • contests • midnight supper • active sports (see alternatives) • pinatas

Themes: western, Mexican, luau, hat, pot luck, barbecue, roller skating, ice skating, speaker, celebrity, scavenger hunt.

---

*Developed by Parents Who Care, Inc., California Bay Area.

Location Of Party

- Where will the party be held? Are the facilities appropriate for the activities and adequate for the number of people? What equipment is lacking or needed? Indoor? Outdoor? Parking?

Guests

- How many? Is the number right for the facility and the activities? Is the group compatible with the kind of party?

Invitations

- Should include: Kind of party, activities, date, time, place, if meal is being served, special information, appropriate dress.
- Hours: Do they fit activities? Are they appropriate for the age group?
- Should guests bring anything? food, games, costume, present, bathing suit, towel, etc.?

Decorations

- What decorations are appropriate for type of party and/or the theme?
- Equipment needed? tables, chairs, flowers, hurricane lamps, indoor-outdoor lighting, table cloths, posters, special effects, etc.?

Food And Drink Preparation

All possible preparation should be done in advance. Food should be simple, and what teenagers like. Guests may be asked to bring food.

- Plan menu — when guests arrive, meal, ongoing snacks, desserts, whatever is appropriate. Remember things like salt, pepper, dressings, garnishes.
- Plan equipment needed — serving dishes and utensils, eating dishes and utensils, preparing and cooking dishes and utensils — also special equipment (e.g., barbecue), napkins, etc.
- Purchase food (watch ads for food specials). Drinks should be provided in abundance (soft drinks, lemonade, punch, iced tea, etc.).
- Have plenty of ice, bottle openers, glasses.
- Provisions for refuse should be made and apparent.

Schedule And Planning Of Activities

- Plan a schedule of how the party's activities will flow.

    Plan to keep things moving.

    Be willing to be flexible.

    What will be happening when people arrive? Plan an icebreaker.

- Planning of activities:

    Be sure you have all of the equipment needed for each activity planned (purchased, borrowed)

    Have everything set up and ready to go.

What you can expect if your child's arrested

By Carol Boigon

Sometimes it's a can of beer in the back seat. Sometimes it's a shoving match at a teen gathering place. Or it might be a romantic rendezvous in the park after closing.

Suddenly, that nice boy who mows the lawn or the sweet little girl who used to babysit before her social calendar filled is facing a police officer explaining charges.

Nothing quite equals the tension of the cop's phone call to parents. Very little prepares those mothers and fathers for a run-in with the forces of public order.

The Aurora prosecutors' office has a standard procedure for first-time offenders, a procedure parents would do well to understand.

According to managing prosecutor Clay Douglas, the city offers each first timer a bargain: plead guilty and take a deferred judgment. Keep out of trouble for six months, give or take a traffic ticket, and the city will withdraw the plea, drop the charges and wipe the record clean.

If no evidence substantiates the charge, the case will be dismissed, Douglas said. Plea-bargained probation is not offered to those with a criminal record or those charged with serious crimes.

Douglas's assistant, prosecutor David Beard, said city attorneys also consider the wishes of victims and the presence of injuries in deciding whether to propose a deferred judgment.

As Beard explained, parents typically respond in one of three ways during a pretrial conference. Some say "I'm only here because the law says I have to be. You work this out with my kid." Others admit the youth's guilt and a desire to protect the child from a criminal record.

Sometimes prosecutors may propose an anti-shoplifting school or alcohol abuse class. Sometimes they suggest a tour of the jail or visits to a probation officer. If an agreement is reached, the offender pleads "guilty" and gets a deferred judgment and probation. If the terms are met, he or she walks away without a criminal record.

But some parents believe their children's claims of innocence. What do they say to their children who proclaim total innocence. Do they tell the youths to lie and plead guilty? Or do they hire a lawyer and gamble on a judge or jury agreeing with the family's version of events?

Prosecutors may reveal some evidence, but if parents don't reconsider, the case will go to trial.

THAT'S THE MIDDLE of the story. Here's how it starts, for an imaginary Susie. A clerk at Sears thinks 16-year-old Susie Q stole a lipstick. Store security people hold her until a police officer arrives.

The officer learns sweet Sue is under 18 and takes her to the Aurora police station. If she were older, the officer could choose to simply issue a summons.

From the station, the officer calls Susie's dad who races over to the jail. Mr. Q signs a promise to appear in court with his daughter because, by law, she can't even plead not guilty for herself until she turns 18.

Mr. Q is told the charges — shoplifting — and a date is set for her arraignment.

The arraignment is Susie's chance to tell the court her plea: guilty, not guilty or no contest. If she pleads guilty or no contest the judge will sentence her or call for a "pre-sentencing investigation." The investigation consists of a probation officer evaluating measures that would best steer Sue away from a life of misdemeanors.

If Susie pleads not guilty, she and her folks may ask to talk with the city attorney. At the arraignment, the judge will ask Sue's parents whether she wants a trial to a judge or to a jury. Or whether she'd like a pretrial conference with a prosecutor.

"It's the one time they'll get to discuss the possibilities informally," Beard said. "Sometimes parents mistakenly believe in their kids' innocence.

The prosecutor shows a clip of Susie's pink-lace-gloved hand slipping Max Factor's mulberry into her aqua shoulder bag. Sears can film every customer in the store, with close-ups and travel shots.

Now Daddy's convinced; Sue's chagrined.

The three agree Sue will pay the $30 costs of six month probation out of her babysitting money, see the probation officer once a month for six months and stay out of trouble.

She pleads guilty and gets sentenced to a deferred judgment and six months probation. Susie is a good girl who learned her lesson: 180 days later she walks away from the incident without leaving a fingerprint. As of late, she's been seen paying for her cosmetics.

POTENTIAL LEGAL LIABILITIES OF THE "KEGGER" SCENARIO

The following breakdown is not meant as an example of what charges would in fact be brought, but more, what the potential charges available to the District Attorney are, based on the fact pattern presented.

Planning, Setting Up Party, Sale of Liquor

- Potential parental liability regarding sale of liquor. This includes parents of the 18 year olds as well as the 16 year old "host" although presumably they were out of town. If the parents knew of and acquiesced in the party or gave explicit permission, then there is direct liability under the Liquor Code.

  For permitting persons under 21 to consume alcohol "under conditions which an average person should have knowledge of."
  Misdemeanor

  Complicity liability if parents consented to and helped plan, promote or facilitate the offense. *Misdemeanor*

- Liability of the liquor seller

  Could lose liquor license; also

  Subject to liability for selling liquor to a minor under Liquor Code provisions. *Misdemeanor*

- Potential liability of 18 year olds (but less than 21). 18 year olds are treated as adults under the Childrens' Code.

  For obtaining liquor by misrepresenting age. *Misdemeanor*

  For selling liquor to children under 21. *Misdemeanor*

  For selling or serving liquor to an obviously intoxicated person, some under 21 years of age or a known drunkard. *Misdemeanor*

  For contributing to the delinquency of a minor. *Class 4 Felony*

- Potential liability of those under 18 years old. Adolescents under 18 years old are treated as children under the Children's Code and "diverted" into the Juvenile Law System. The possible actions facing them are:

  Being taken into custody.

  Referral to the District Attorney for further action if appropriate.

  A "Petition in Delinquency" filed by the District Attorney.

  Referral to the appropriate social agency for counselling.

---

*Developed by H. Michael Steinberg, Deputy District Attorney, Arapahoe County, Colorado.

Party In Progress

- Regarding sale or supply of Jack Daniels — 18 years or older.

    Potential liability under the Liquor Code   *Misdemeanor*

    Potential liability for contributing to the delinquency of a minor.
    Class 4 Felony

- Regarding sale of marijuana — 18 years or older.

    For selling more than one ounce to a child under 18 but at least 15.
    Class 4 Felony

    Second offense.   *Class 3 Felony*

- Regarding sale of marijuana where seller is under 18.

    The offender is diverted to the Juvenile System.

- Regarding the fight between the 2 boys. The parents are immune from civil liability for the personal injuries to each of the children unless the parents knew that:

    The child had a propensity to commit the abuse.

    The parent had knowledge of the propensity, and

    The parent failed to stop the child from committing the act.

    The parents cannot be held criminally liable unless there was aiding and abetting of the crime or some conspiracy afoot —neither of which is hinted at in this scenario.

- Regarding the fight between the two boys — when they are over 18. Each child could be charged with:

    Assault in the third degree.   *Misdemeanor*

    Criminal Mischief — depending on damages.
    Class 3 Misdemeanor to Class 3 Felony

    Disorderly Conduct.   *Class 3 Misdemeanor*

    NOTE: The Court has the authority to order restitution as a condition of probation under [16-11-204.5]. The Court could order students to pay for actual damages they have done.

- Regarding the fight if both children under 18.

    They are diverted into the Juvenile Law System.

- Potential parental liability for property damage. A property owner can sue a parent civilly for up to $3,500 for the damages done by that parent's child where that child "maliciously or willfully destroys property."

Other Potential Crimes Chargeable

- Criminal Trespass

    1st Degree — knowingly and unlawfully entering or remaining in a dwelling with intent to steal a valuable item.   *Class 5 Felony*

2nd Degree — unlawful entering upon premises enclosed in a manner designed to exclude intruders (e.g. fenced yard) or knowingly and unlawfully remaining in a hotel, condominium, or apartment building *Class 3 Misdemeanor*

3rd Degree — unlawfully entering and remaining on premises (such as real property, buildings or other improvements).
Class 1 Petty Offense

- Resisting Arrest

    Creating a substantial risk of bodily injury to a police officer.
    Class 3 Misdemeanor

- Obstructing a Police Officer

    Using or threatening to use violence, force or physical interference to unknowingly obstruct or hinder a law enforcement official in the preservation of the peace.

    NOTE: This is true even if the arrest is an illegal arrest.
    Class 2 Misdemeanor

- Accessory to a Crime

    If with intent to hinder, delay, or prevent the discovery, detection, apprehension, prosecution, conviction or punishment — or renders assistance to a suspected criminal by harboring, concealing, warning, aiding the escape, threatening others who help, or by concealing evidence.

    Depending upon the danger of the criminal one is aiding.
    Class 1 Petty Offense to Class 4 Felony

- Refusing to Aid a Police Officer

    A person 18 years or older, who, when commanded, unreasonably refuses to aid a peace officer in the arrest or prevention of a crime.
    Class 1 Petty Offense

- Harassment

    If with intent to harass, annoy, or alarm a person strikes, shoves, kicks, touches, or publicly directs obscene language or gestures (a pattern of acts calculated to annoy). *Class 3 Misdemeanor*

- Failure or Refusal to leave Premises or Property at the Request of a Police Officer.

    The refusal or barricading of police entry to any premises through the use of or threatened use of force. *Class 3 Misdemeanor*

    The refusal to leave an area upon request by a police officer who suspects a crime is occurring and the person's refusal to leave is a danger to the police and others. *Class 3 Misdemeanor*

- Reckless Endangerment

    A person who recklessly engages in conduct which creates a substantial risk of serious bodily injury to another.

    Class 3 Misdemeanor

- Fraudulent Proof of Age

    It is unlawful for any person to obtain any fermented malt beverage by misrepresentation of age or by any oher method in any place where fermented malt beverages are sold if such person is under eighteen years of age. **Misdemeanor**

Unlawful Acts Statute (Liquor Code Penalties)

Unlike any other law the Unlawful Acts Statute has its own penalties built into it. Depending on the violation, the sentence falls into one of two categories:

- Class A: $5,000 maximum fine; 12 months maximum jail or both.
- Class B: $500 maximum fine; 3 months maximum jail.

APPENDIX H

WIIS

Western Insurance Information Service

6000 East Evans Avenue, Building 2, Suite 333
Denver, CO 80222 (303) 759-2892

An Open Letter to Parents and Teenage Drivers
from Western Insurance Information Service

It's Saturday night and your 16-year-old armed with a recently issued driver's license borrows the family car to taxi friends to their weekly pizza and Pacman ritual. On their way home at midnight, your teenager loses control of the vehicle and crashes head-on into another car. No one will ever know why the fatal swerve was made, and no one lived to tell the story.

The above scenario is a tragic one, and unfortunately, not all that uncommon. Thousands of teenagers are involved in traffic accidents each year.. thousands! And a large percentage of these accidents are alcohol related.

Teen arrests for drunk driving have more than tripled since 1980. Statistics also show that a teenager is 2½ to 3 times more likely to be in a fatal accident involving alcohol than other drivers.

<u>Drunk driving is a crime</u>. It is unlawful for any person who is considered under the influence of alcohol to drive a vehicle. If convicted, it is an offense that stays on your driving record for seven years and in most cases affects your insurance rates dramatically for three to five years. Insurance companies look at these records routinely before renewal to evaluate policyholder's driving performance and to determine insurance rates. If you are convicted of a DUI (<u>d</u>riving <u>u</u>nder the <u>i</u>nfluence of alcohol), insurance companies will check your records more often than others who do not have violations or convictions. In DUI cases where a driver's license has been suspended, most insurance companies will automatically cancel a policy, since you cannot obtain insurance without a valid driver's license. This forces first time offenders upon renewal of their license to look elsewhere for insurance, and at a <u>much higher rate</u>.

Naturally, violation-free drivers don't pay the same rates as those who have frequent violations. So, in a general sense a policyholder makes his own rates and, in the case of a drunk driving conviction, it's almost a certainty that the higher you get, the higher your premiums will rise!

Keep in mind too, that when you are convicted of a DUI, you place your entire family's insurance coverage in jeopardy as well.

Here's an example of how insurance premiums for a two-car family living in a mid-western metropolitan community would be affected if the father or teenage son were convicted of drunken driving.*

    Mr. and Mrs. John Williams drive a 1983 Oldsmobile Cutlass and their son, Tim, 18, drives a 1982 Chevette. The Williams' policy is typical of the auto coverage bought by many families; i.e: $100,000 liability for bodily injury/property damage; comprehensive coverage with a $50 deductible; and collision insurance with a $200 deductible. Since all members have clean driving records, coverage for the Cutlass comes to $579.80 annually, while coverage for the Chevette, Tim's car, totals $1,598.60 per year.** The family is paying out a total of $2,178.40 in premiums annually.

If 18-year-old Tim were convicted of a DUI, his insurance costs would jump to $2,490.60 and in turn affect the rates of his parents' car as well, causing the premium on the Cutlass to rise to $661.60. This brings the total household premium to $3,152.20 per year. In summary, one DUI conviction resulted in a nearly 70 percent hike in annual rates for the entire household. With close to $1,000 in insurance premiums due each year, or roughly $80 extra a month, Tim's parents could find his DUI a costly one.

If both Mr. Williams and his son were convicted of a DUI, Mr. Williams' premium would rise to $1,322.20 and with the cost for his son's car at $2,490.60, total household premiums would reach $3,812.80. Two DUI convictions in one household nearly doubled the cost of insurance.

At this point the Williams' insurance agent could choose to cancel their policy or refer then to an Assigned Risk Plan, which would amount to a threefold increase over their rates with clean driving records.

For the Williams another option exists...they can buy insurance from a specialty risk carrier; but they can expect even higher rates than the Assigned Risk Plan. In any case every state has either a financial responsibility law or compulsory auto insurance law. Many have both. Even where ownership of insurance is not compulsory, the existence of the financial responsibility laws, along with the threat of a financially crippling judgment in the event of an accident, has come to make the possession of auto liability insurance a virtual necessity for most motorists.

As a final and somewhat extreme example, the following actual case was provided from an insurance company's claim file. It illustrates the financial impact a drunk driver can have on his or her insurance company.

In this case, the insured, driving under the influence of alcohol, collided with two cars then struck a guard rail. One person was killed and another slightly injured. The insured was not hurt. Insurance costs are as follows: physical damage costs (one car repair and guard rail) - $13,194; bodily injury costs (one fatality, medical costs, legal and investigative fees) - $455,767. Grand total insurance costs - $458,961.

Let's take this case one step further and create a scenario where this insured was your teenager's friend, leaving a party that was given at your home with your knowledge.

In September, 1984, the New Jersey Supreme Court ruled that anyone serving liquor in his or her home could be held liable if an intoxicated guest drives away and subsequently is involved in an accident. In this case, as the host of the party, you could ultimately be held responsible for this accident.

Most homeowners policies have a liability limit of $100,000; however in this case, where damages are greater than this amount, personal

APPENDIX H

assets can come into play; and worse yet, your liability insurance does not cover punitive damages - money awarded by a jury beyond actual loss as punishment for irresponsible actions. Because of the nature of these claims, insurance companies are researching whether underwriters need to take into consideration the amount of entertaining families do. Parents are now apt to check homeowner liability more closely to reexamine coverage limits.

In any case, it is advisable to check with your insurance agent and discuss liability coverage as it relates to you as parents hosting a party, your teenager, or if your teenager co-hosts a party with friends at their homes.

While the insured in this scenario will have to pay a substantially high premium for their insurance in the future, the vast majority of the cost their accident will be borne by other drivers. Through the principle of surance, those costs are distributed among other insureds who never have had or will have an accident. This makes the drunk driver not only a men to other highway users, but a financial burden to everyone who buys auto bile insurance.

*Insurance rates cited in this hypothetical situation were obtained fro an insurance company and do not necessarily reflect the rates charged other insurance companies.

**National Safety Council studies and insurance industry experience indi cate that drivers aged 15-19 years have a much higher accident freque and that the average coverage cost of their claims is substantially higher, thus the premiums are higher. From 19-25 years insurance rate drop only slightly.

PLEASE REMEMBER YOUR RESPONSIBILITY - TO YOURSELF,
YOUR FAMILY AND THE LIVES OF OTHERS.
THINK - BEFORE YOU START DRINKING!

CW/cp
8/86

(Western Insurance Information Service is a non-profit, consumer educati organization supported by the property-casualty insurance industry.)

SAMPLE CONTINGENCY CONTRACT

Of _____
                   (Name of Teenager)

I am changing my lifestyle. I will not go to the following places:

1. _____ 2. _____

I am changing my friends. These are the people I will not call or see:

1. _____ 2. _____

If I call/see any of the above people, I will take the following consequences:

1. _____ 2. _____

These are the friends and acquaintances I will spend time with:

1. _____ 2. _____

These are the time limits I am setting for myself:

   1. I will be in the house at _____ Sundays through Thursdays.

   2. I will be in the house at _____ Friday and Saturday.

   3. I will be awake and out of bed at _____ on weekdays.

   4. I will be awake and out of bed at _____ on weekends.

If I'm irresponsible and don't follow these limits, these will be my consequences:

1. _____ 2. _____

When I go out:

   1. I will inform my parents:
      Where I am going, check it out, and get permission.
      Who is providing the transportation.
      Who I am going to be with.
      When I plan to return.

   2. I will call if I change locations.

   3. If I have to go out before my parents return home I will leave a note as to my whereabouts and approximate time of return.

   4. I will put a calendar of all upcoming events in a prominent place.

If I do not follow the above requirements, these are my consequences:

1. _____ 2. _____

These jobs at home, must be completed before I am entitled to any privileges:

1. _____ Daily ____ Weekly ____ As Needed ____

2. _____ Daily ____ Weekly ____ As Needed ____

I will not need to be reminded and will do my work thoroughly!

If I do not follow through with the above agreement, these are my consequences:

1. _____ 2. _____

      SIGNED: _____
                                 (Teenager)

                     _____
                                    (Parent)

CHERRY CREEK SCHOOL DISTRICT SUBSTANCE ABUSE POLICY AND PROCEDURE

Student Use and Abuse of Alcohol, Marijuana, Other Controlled Substances

POLICY 5123

School personnel have an ethical commitment and an obligation to students, community, and profession. They must be concerned with the mental, physical, and emotional development of each student. In viewing this concern and accompanying duties, educators must balance the rights of the individual student with those of the society in which the student lives.

The Board expects the development and implementation of educational programs which will have a positive effect upon student values, provide information on the harmful effects of dangerous drugs, and aid in the prevention of drug/alcohol abuse. Such educational programs shall be subject to frequent revision in order to be current with new research and information that becomes available.

The Board supports the concept that parents have the responsibility to cooperate with the school in attempting to prevent problems of drug/alcohol abuse and to seek help from public and private agencies for students who become involved with drug/alcohol abuse. In this regard, whenever possible, in dealing with student problems associated with drug/alcohol abuse, school personnel will provide parents and students with the information concerning educational and rehabilitation programs that are available in the area.

The Board supports the concept that staff members have the responsibility to consistently enforce this policy; further, that school personnel be exposed to the most recent research and information available with respect to the hazards of drug/alcohol use.

Being under the influence of, using/possessing, distributing, selling, giving, or exchanging alcohol, marijuana, or other controlled substances (as defined in the Colorado Controlled Substance Act of 1981, C. R. S. 12-22-301 et seq.) or drug paraphernalia is prohibited because it constitutes a hazard in all Cherry Creek Schools, on school grounds, at school-sanctioned activities, or when students are being transported in vehicles dispatched by the district or waiting at bus stops.

The enforcement of this policy shall be in keeping with the applicable Colorado Statutes and the administrative procedures adopted pursuant hereto, which statutes and procedures shall be followed by all Cherry Creek personnel.

To insure the enforcement of this policy, general and specific searches shall be authorized to the extent and upon the grounds permitted by law, and shall be conducted in accord with the administrative procedures adopted pursuant to this policy.

Nothing contained in the foregoing Policy shall be construed to extend or expand the School District's duty to supervise or control students or areas within School District jurisdiction beyond that which existed under law prior to the adoption of the foregoing Policy.

PROCEDURE 5123-1

A. **Introduction**

In administering Policy 5123, the following procedures will be strictly observed.

B. **Definitions**

1. *Controlled Substances*

   a. Controlled substances shall be substances as defined in the Colorado Controlled Substance Act of 1981, (C.R.S. 12-22-301, et seq.).
   b. Controlled substances shall include, but not be limited to cocaine, heroin, alcohol and marijuana.

2. *Within School District Jurisdiction*

   A student will be considered within the School District's jurisdiction when: on school grounds, at school-sanctioned activities, when being transported in vehicles dispatched by the District or waiting at bus stops.

3. *Under the Influence*

   A student shall be considered under the influence when his/her comportment, behavior, condition, speech or appearance, while within School District jurisdiction, is affected by, or evinces, the prior use of a controlled substance.

4. *Use or Possession*

   A student shall be considered using or possessing a controlled substance or drug paraphernalia if the controlled substance or drug paraphernalia is found: on one's person, personal property, car or other vehicle, locker, desk or other storage area within the District's jurisdiction.

5. *Drug Paraphernalia*

   Drug paraphernalia shall be any machine, instrument, tool or device which is primarily designed and intended for one or more of the following:

   a. to introduce into the human body; and/or
   b. to enhance the effect on the human body of; and/or
   c. to conceal any quantity of; and/or
   d. to test the strength, effectiveness or purity of any controlled substances under circumstances in violation of the law of Colorado.

6. *Counterfeit Drugs*

   Counterfeit drugs are any substance which is represented as a controlled substance, also known as Turkey drugs or look alikes.

7. *Distributing, Selling, Giving or Exchanging*

   This is any means by which a controlled substance is dispensed from one to another.

C. **Transfer of Records**

   Records of substantiated controlled substance offenses, noting date, type of offense, and disciplinary action taken will be maintained at the building level and will be forwarded to the appropriate administrator of discipline at the next level or school the student attends in the District. These records will be confidential. Keeping records is not meant to be punitive but rather an aid to school authorities tracking case histories and to be aware of situations that may need attention.

D. **Disciplinary Action**

   Students shall be subject to disciplinary action up to and including suspension and expulsion, for being under the influence of, using, possessing, distributing, selling, giving or exchanging controlled substances, drug paraphernalia or counterfeit drugs. Due process, as stipulated in District Policy 5114 shall be followed in suspensions or expulsions.

   If a handicapped student who is receiving special education services, is involved with any of the specified offenses, regular disciplinary action may be taken. The student's Individual Education Program (IEP) will be reviewed by the IEP staffing team prior to/at the same time disciplinary action is being taken. A copy of the disciplinary referral form completed by the school administrator will be placed in the student's cumulative record.

   All offenses will be subject to the provisions of the disciplinary actions listed. Such offenses may be in a single category or a combination of all categories when compiling cumulative offenses.

   All staff members will cooperate fully with appropriate law enforcement investigators relative to students being under the influence of using, possessing, distributing, selling, giving or exchanging controlled substances.

   1. *Under the Influence*

      The following procedures are to be followed for students under the influence of controlled substances while within the School District's jurisdiction:

      a. If a student appears to be under the influence due to the possibility of having used a controlled substance, the staff member will notify the building principal or designee who will observe the student.

      b. When necessary, individual school emergency procedures will be followed.

      c. If it is determined by the principal, or principal's designee, that the unusual behavior may be due to the student being under the

influence, parents will be contacted as soon as possible. When contacting parents, they are to be advised that their student is displaying unusual or dangerous behavior. The behavior is to be described, but no attempt to diagnose the student's condition will be made.
d. While waiting for the parent or medical aid, if applicable, the student will not be left alone, but will be placed in a quiet situation where the student will remain under observation.
e. If it is determined that the student is under the influence, the student will be subject to the provisions below.
f. Contact with legal authorities may result and the parents and student will be notified of this contact.

First Offense:

(1) The student will be suspended for a minimum of one (1) and a maximum of five (5) school days.
(2) A parent conference will be held before the student is readmitted to school.
(3) The school official will attempt to develop with the parents and the student, written agreement that will outline the responsibilities of the parent, the student, and the school in an effort to keep any further offenses from occurring. This agreement will specifically state consequences of a second offense.
(4) Parents and students will be provided information concerning voluntary drug and alcohol treatment counselling programs.

Second Offense:

Repeat (1) and (2) as outlined under First Offense.
(3) Information concerning voluntary drug or alcohol treatment programs will be given to students and parents.
(4) Written evidence of participation in appropriate rehabilitation programs will influence consequences of this second offense.
(5) A written agreement will be completed with school official, student and parents indicating that expulsion may be the result of a third offense.
(6) Where circumstances warrant, special consideration for an In-district transfer will be considered, as well as other educational alternatives.
An In-district transfer requires the mutual agreement of the Administrators of the two schools involved. Transportation to the new school will be the responsibility of the student and parents.

Third Offense:

(1) The student will be suspended until the expulsion hearing takes place.

(2) Procedures to be followed for requesting an expulsion from school are outlined.
(3) If the student participates in an appropriate rehabilitation or treatment program, as evidenced by a written statement and recommendation for readmittance from the source of the rehabilitation or treatment program is presented, the District will consider readmittance to school at the end of the semester.
(4) If (3) is not achieved, the expulsion shall remain in effect for the balance of the current school year.
(5) At the end of the year, depending on circumstances and the judgment of school authorities, the student may return to school or be given an In-district transfer.

2. *Use or Possession*

The following procedures are to be followed for students who use or possess controlled substances, or drug paraphernalia while within the School District's jurisdiction will be handled in the following manner:

a. A school staff member who comes in contact with drug paraphernalia and/or controlled substances will notify the building administrator immediately.
b. A school staff member who has reasonable cause to believe that a student is in possession of controlled substances or drug paraphernalia will immediately attempt to detain the student and request that he/she accompany the staff member to the principal or designee. If the student refuses, the staff member will notify the principal or designee immediately. If this occurs, the staff member should make every effort to remain with the student, while using other means to contact the principal or principal's designee.
c. The principal or designee will attempt to obtain evidence by directly requesting it from the student or through search procedures that are outlined.
d. If the substance is suspected to be a controlled substance, the principal or principal's designee may have the evidence tested to determine its contents. The principal or designee will then place the evidence in an envelope. The envelope will be sealed, dated, and initialed by the individual who originally obtained the materials and the principal or designee, and then placed in the school safe.
e. The principal or designee will call the appropriate law enforcement agency and request that an officer pick up the sealed envelope containing the substance.
f. If testing shows that the substance is a controlled substance, or if the student admits in writing, to it being a controlled substance the principal or principal's designee shall take the disciplinary action as outlined below:

First Offense:

(1) The student will be suspended for a minimum of one (1) and a maximum of five (5) school days. Legal authorities may be contacted.
(2) A parent conference will be held before the student is readmitted to school.
(3) The school official will attempt to develop with the parents and the student, written agreement that will outline the responsibilities of the parent, the student, and the school in an effort to keep any further offenses from occurring. This agreement will specifically state consequences of a second offense.
(4) Parents and students will be provided information concerning voluntary drug and alcohol treatment counselling programs.

Second Offense:

Repeat (1) and (2) as outlined under First Offense.
(3) Information concerning voluntary drug and/or alcohol treatment programs will be given to students and parents.
(4) Written evidence of participation in appropriate rehabilitation programs will influence consequences of this second offense.
(5) A written agreement will be complete with school official, student and parents indicating that expulsion may be the result of a third offense.
(6) Where circumstances warrant, special consideration for an In-district transfer will be considered, as well as other educational alternatives.
An In-district transfer requires the mutual agreement of the Administrators of the two schools involved. Transportation to the new school will be the responsibility of the student and parents.

Third Offense:

(1) The student will be suspended until the expulsion hearing takes place.
(2) Procedures to be followed for requesting an expulsion from school are outlined.
(3) If the student participates in an appropriate rehabilitation or treatment program, as evidenced by a written statement and recommendation for readmittance from the source of the rehabilitation or treatment program is presented, the District will consider readmittance to school at the end of the semester.
(4) If (3) is not achieved, the expulsion shall remain in effect for the balance of the current school year.
(5) At the end of the year, depending on circumstances and the judgment of school authorities, the student may return to school or be given an In-district transfer.

3. *Distributing, Selling, Giving, or Exchanging*

The following procedures are to be followed for students who are engaged in distributing, selling, giving, or exchanging controlled substances, drug paraphernalia or counterfeit drugs while within the School District's jurisdiction:

a. If a staff member is a witness to an act in which suspected controlled substances, drug paraphernalia, or counterfeit drugs are being distributed, sold, given, or exchanged from one student to another, the staff member will immediately attempt to detain the student and request that he/she accompany him/her to the principal or designee. If the student refuses, the staff member will notify the principal or designee immediately. If this occurs, the staff member should make every effort to remain with the student, while using other means to contact the principal or principal's designee.
b. The principal or designee will attempt to obtain evidence by directly requesting it from the student of through search procedures as outlined.
c. If the substance is suspected to be a controlled substance, the principal or principal's designee may have the evidence tested to determine its contents. The principal or designee will then place the evidence in an envelope. The envelope will be sealed, dated, and initialed by the principal or designee, and then placed in the school safe.
d. The principal or designee will call the appropriate law enforcement agency and request that an officer pick up the sealed envelope containing the substance.
e. If testing shows that the substance is a controlled substance, or if the student admits in writing to one of the above, the principal or principal's designee shall take the disciplinary action as outlined below:

First Offense:

(1) The student will be suspended from school for a minimum of three (3) and a maximum of five (5) school days. Legal authorities may be contacted.
(2) The principal or designee will conduct a conference with the parent, student, and if possible, a law enforcement representative prior to the student being readmitted to school. A written agreement between school official, parent and the student will be completed indicating that expulsion may result on the second offense.
(3) Depending on the severity of the case, the principal may initiate procedures outlined in Policy 5114, which may lead to a request to the Superintendent of Schools, and ultimately to the Board of Education, for expulsion of the student.

Second Offense:

(1) A recommendation for expulsion will result in substan-

tiated cases upon the second offense. The length of the expulsion will be determined by considering the student's age and personal situation.

(2) Procedures to be followed for requesting an expulsion from school are outlined in Policy 5114.

E. **Searches**

1. *Locker/Desk/Storage Area Searches*

   All lockers and other storage areas provided for student use on school premises remain the property of the school district and are provided for the use of the students subject to inspection, access for maintenance and search pursuant to this policy. No student shall lock or otherwise impede access to any locker or storage area except with a lock provided by or approved by the principal of the school in which the locker or storage area is located. Unapproved locks shall be removed and destroyed.

   a. The principal, or designee, may authorize the search of a locker and its contents when there is reasonable cause to suspect discovery of prohibited items.
   b. The principal, designee, or a teacher may authorize the search of a desk or any other storage area on school premises, other than a locker when the person conducting the search has reasonable cause to suspect discovery of prohibited items.
   c. A principal, or his designee, may authorize a general search at any time, of all or a portion of the lockers, desks, or other storage areas as a matter of course without notice to the student body.

2. *Personal Searches*

   The principal, or designee, may authorize the search of the person of a student if there is reasonable cause to suspect discovery of prohibited items. The parent or guardian of any student searched under this provision shall be informed of the search as soon as reasonably possible.

   Searches of the person of a student shall be limited to:

   a. Searches of the clothing of the student.
   b. Any object of whatsoever kind or nature in the possession of the student, including but not limited to, purse, briefcase, or backpack.

2. *Motor Vehicle Searches*

   Students by virtue of having the privilege of parking a motor vehicle on school property are deemed to have given prior consent for search of a motor vehicle that has been brought by the student onto school premises.

   The principal, or member of the administrative staff, may authorize the search of a motor vehicle on school premises, if there is a reasonable cause to suspect prohibited items. (See involvement of Law Enforcement Officers.)

F. **Custody of Evidence**

Anything found in the course of a search conducted in accordance with this section which is evidence of a violation of school rules and regulations may be:

1. Seized, tested, and/or admitted as evidence in any suspension or expulsion proceeding. If testing of a substance by a District Administrator, or designee, has shown it to be a controlled substance, and if the substance has been turned over to a law enforcement agency, written documentation or the identification of the substance will be maintained and admitted as evidence in any suspension or expulsion proceeding.
2. Turned over to a law enforcement officer shall be in accordance with the subsection entitled "Involvement of Law Enforcement Officers."

G. **Involvement of Law Enforcement Officers**

The principal, or designee, may request the assistance of a law enforcement officer to:

1. Conduct a search of school property, including lockers, desks and other storage areas.
2. Conduct a search of any motor vehicle or any object in the possession of the student, such as a purse, briefcase or backpack, if the student refuses to permit school authorities to conduct such a search. In the case of such refusal, the principal or assistant principal shall first attempt to contact and secure assistance of the student's parent before involving a law enforcement officer.
3. Identify or take possession of prohibited items found in the course of a search conducted in accordance with this section.
4. Before involving a law enforcement officer in any search in the absence of probable cause of discovery of prohibited items, the principal or his designee shall obtain from the law enforcement officer a commitment that any items secured in the search will not be used in a criminal or juvenile proceeding against the student. Where probable cause of discovery does exist, no such commitment need be obtained. The determination as to the existence of probable cause shall be left to the law enforcement officer and judiciary.

H. Nothing contained in the foregoing Administrative Procedure shall be construed to extend or expand the School District's duty to supervise or control students or areas within School District jurisdiction beyond that which existed under law prior to the approval of the foregoing Administrative Procedure.

… APPENDIX K | 171

ADDITIONAL RESOURCES AND READING

National Parent Organizations

Families in Action
3845 North Druid Hills Road, Suite 300
Decatur, Georgia 30333   Telephone: 1-404-325-5799

FIA has available for $10 a 164-page manual by Sue Rusche entitled *How to Form a Families in Action Group in Your Community.*

National Federation of Parents for Drug-Free Youth (NFP)
8730 Georgia Avenue, Suite 200
Silver Spring, Maryland 20910   Telephone: 1-800-544-KIDS
(Toll-free)

Individual memberships costing $15 per year include "How to Start a Parent Group in Your Community" plus several other educational brochures for parents and teens. Members also receive a quarterly newsletter, "Prevention Parentline," and regular legislatie updates. Many other valuable materials are available.

Parent Resource Institute on Drug Education (PRIDE)
100 Edgewood Avenue, Suite 1216
Atlanta, Georgia 30303   Telephone: 1-800-2471-7946
(Toll-free)

PRIDE also has a quarterly newsletter and maintains a library of films, slide shows, tapes, conference proceedings and printed materials. Contact PRIDE for a list of available resources.

National Self-Help Groups

Alcoholics Anonymous World Services, Inc.
Box 459, Grand Central Station
New York, New York 10163

Al-Anon and Alateen
AFG, Inc.
P.O. Box 862, Mid-Town Station
New York, New York 10018-0862

Narcotics Anonymous World Services Office, Inc.
P.O. Box 622
Sun Valley, California 91352

AA and NA members are self-styled experts in the drug/alcohol dependence and recovery process. Al-Anon and Alateen are support groups for the relatives and friends of problem drinkers. Some publications are available to the public. Local groups, if available, are listed in the telephone directory.

National Sources of Information, Publications, Etc.

National Clearing House for Alcohol Information
National Institute on Alcohol Abuse and Alcoholism
1776 East Jefferson Street, 4th Floor
Rockville, Maryland 20852

National Council on Alcoholism
733 Third Avenue
New York, New York 10017

National Clearing House for Drug Abuse Information
The National Institute on Drug Abuse
Room 10A56 Parklawn Building
5600 Fishers Lane
Rockville, Maryland 20857

The American Council for Drug Education
5820 Hubbard Drive
Rockville, Maryland 20852

American Lung Association
1740 Broadway
New York, New York 10019

Toll-Free Lines for Drug Information

Alcohol and Drug Helpline	1-800-252-6465
Clearing House Prevention Line Office of Health Information	1-800-336-4797
Cocaine (and "crack")	1-800-COCAINE
	1-800-662-HELP
"Just Say No"	1-800-258-2766
NFP Drug Information Line	1-800-554-KIDS
NIDA Prevention Information Line	1-800-638-2045
PRIDE Drug Information Line	1-800-241-9746

These national lines can provide drug information as well as information regarding sources of help available in your area (organizations, state agencies, treatment services, etc.). Local hot-lines may be listed in the front of your telephone directory white pages under "Community Agencies." Other local sources of help to call are listed in the yellow pages under "Alcoholism" and "Drug Abuse." In a life-threatening crisis situation, call your local hospital emergency room.

SUGGESTED READING MATERIAL

On Alcohol, Marijuana, Cocaine and Other Drugs

800-COCAINE, Mark S. Gold, M.D., Bantam Books, New York, New York

Drugs, Drinking and Adolescents, Donald Ian Macdonald, M.D., Year Book Medical Publishers, Inc., Chicago, Illinois.

Getting Tough on Gateway Drugs: A Guide for the Family, Robert L. Dupont, M.D., American Psychiatric Press, Washington, DC.

Gone Way Down: Teenage Drug-Use is a Disease, Miller Newton, Ph.D., American Studies Press, Tampa, Florida.

How to Cope with a Teenage Drinker, Dr. Gary Forest, Ballantine Books, New York, New York.

Marijuana Alert, Peggy Mann, McGraw-Hill, New York, New York.

Parents, Peers and Pot, Marsha Manatt, Ph.D., National Institute on Drug Abuse, Rockville, Maryland. (A single copy may be ordered free of charge.)

The People's Pharmacy — 2, Joe Graedon, Avon Books, New York, New York.

The Purposes of Pleasure: A Reflection on Youth and Drugs, Richard Hawley, Ph.D., The Independent School Press, Wellesley Hills, Massachusetts.

On Parenting in a Drug/Alcohol Oriented Teen Society

Aggressive Adolescents, David E. Dangerfield, DSW, and Michael H. Shaffer, MSW, Professional Training Associates, Tulare, California.

Developing Capable Young People, Stephen Glen, Humansphere, Inc., Hurst, Texas.

How to Talk to Kids About Drugs, Suzanne Fornaciari, Pacific Institute, Bethesda, Maryland.

Peer Pressure Reversal, Sharon Scott, Human Resource Development Press, Inc., Amherst, Massachusetts.

Steering Clear: Helping Your Child Through the High Risk Drug Years, Dorothy Cretcher, Publications for Parents, Dayton, Ohio.

Strengthening the Family, Stephen Glen, Potomac Press, Washington, DC.

Stress and Your Child, Ruth P. Arent, Prentice-Hall, Inc., Englewood Cliffs, New Jersey.

ToughLove, Phyllis and David York and Ted Wachtel, Bantam Books, New York, New York.

Understanding Early Adolescents: A Framework, John P. Hill, The Center for Early Adolescents, Carrboro, North Carolina.

When Junior Highs Invade Your Home, Cliff Schimmels, Fleming H. Revell Company, Power Books, Old Tappan, New Jersey.

On Combatting the Problem

Parents, Peers, and Pot — II: Parents in Action, National Institute on Drug Abuse, Rockville, Maryland. (Single copies may be ordered free of charge.)

A School Answers Back: Responding to Student Drug Use, The American Council for Drug Education, Rockville, Maryland.

WHAT Works: Schools without Drugs, U.S. Department of Education, Washington, DC. (Single copies may be ordered free of charge by calling 1-800-624-0100.)

On Drunk Driving

Arrive Alive: How to Keep Drunk and Pot-High Drivers Off the Highways, Peggy Mann, Woodmere Press, New York, New York.

Contract for Life, Robert Anastas with Kalia Lulow, Pocketbooks, New York, New York. (Robert Anastas is the founder of SADD — Students Against Driving Drunk.)

On Teenage Suicide Prevention

The Courage to Live, Eric Kiev, M. D., Bantam Books, Inc., New York, New York. (A guide to coping with suicidal depression.)

The Urge to Die, Peter Giovacchini, M. D., Publisher, City, State. (A guide to recognizing and coping with suicidal behavior in young people.)

On Teenage Sex

Changing Bodies, Changing Lives, Ruth Bell, Random House, New York, New York.

Miscellaneous Adult Topics

Adult Children of Alcoholics, Janet Geringer Woititz, Ed. D., Health Communications, Inc., Pompano Beach, Florida.

Caring Enough to Confront, David Augsberger, Regal Books, Ventura, California.

Don't Say Yes When You Want to Say No, Herbert Fensterheim, Dell Publishing Co., New York, New York.

Index

A

Absentee parents, keg parties, 48
Abuse, definition of, 101
Abuser, definition of, 103-4
Addiction
　definition of, 104
　signs/symptoms of, 103
Addiction Research and Treatment Service (ARTS), 107, 125
Additional Resources and Reading, 171-2
Adolescent idealism, 16-7
Adolescent personality changes, 15-6
Adolescent stress, 22
Adolescent users compared to other adolescents, 106-7
Adolescents
　peer groups, 14
　typical, characteristics of, 13-8
Advances in Pediatrics, 125
After school beer/pot parties, 45-6
Aftercare
　parent support groups, 131
　peer support groups, 131
　school's role in, 132-3
Aftercare support group, 100
Aftercare treatment, need for, 130-4
Alateen, 133, 138
Alcohol
　as most popular drug among teenagers, 19
　effects when combined with marijuana, 31
　facts about, 24-7
　impairment of driving skills, 70
　legal liabilities, 70
　risks of early use, 67
Alcohol, effects on
　body, 25, 27, 67-8
　brain cells, 24
　driving skills, 25
　judgment, 70
　mental and emotional development, 66-7
　motivation, 69
　school performance, 68-9
　social development, 69
Alcohol abuse, effect on health, 26-7
Alcohol abuse, family's role in prevention, 70-1
Alcohol and drug task force, local, 86
Alcohol and drug use by parents, 78
Alcohol and drug use, parental awareness, 71-81
Alcohol content in various beverages, 25
Alcohol/drug combinations, effect on driving, 39, 59-60
Alcohol/drugs, parental use, 106
Alcoholics Anonymous, 132
Amphetamines, 19
Appendices, 143-174
Arrest, parental response to, 122
Attainable goals, importance of, 78-9
Attorney costs, 141
Authority, parental, 74
　motives in exercising, 72
　resentment toward, 149
Auto insurance rates, effect of drunk driving charges, 62
Awareness Test for Parents, 146-7

B

BAC, blood alcohol concentration, 25, 59
　effect of different levels of, 26
　methods of measuring, 25
Barbiturates, 19
Beer parties, 48-58
　(see also "keg parties")
　after school, 45-6
　alternatives to, 92
　condoned by parents, 46
　police action, 140
　prevention and control, 46
Behavior changes, as symptoms of drug use, 104-5
Bibliography, 173-4
Blood alcohol concentration (BAC), 25, 59
Breathalizer test, 25
Brewster, Tom, 107, 125
Buddy system, 54
BYOB parties, 47
　legal liabilities, 55-6
　popular locations, 52
"Burnout", marijuana, 30-1

C

Cannabis Sativa, (marijuana), 30
Center for Behavioral Medicine, 19
Changes, physical, in adolescents, 15
Checklist for teens, problem situations, 134-6
Chemical patterns for drugs, 38-9
Cherry Creek School District, 120, 162-170
Children of alcoholics, 20
China White, a designer drug, 37
Cigarettes, clove, 28
Civil liabilities
　drunk driving, 60-1
　keg parties, 55
Civil suits, auto accidents, 62
Clove cigarettes, 28
Cocaine, 19, 31-4
　facts about, 31-4
　health problems associated with, 33
Cocaine hotline, 36
Cocaine use, sudden death from, 33-4
Cold and cough remedies, effect on driving skills, 39
Commitment of teenager for treatment, 124
Communication, effective, need for, 80-1
Communication skills, impact of drug/alcohol use on, 22
Community prevention efforts, 85-6
Conflicts, resolving, 81
Conformity neurosis, in adolescents, 14-5
Confronting the advanced user problem, 116
Conning
　behavior, coping with, 89
　by teenagers, 120
Consequences of crack use, 74-5
Consistency, in parents, importance of, 72
Contingency contract, 124, 161

[175]

(contingency contract, continued)
   as method of enforcement, 117-18
Contingency management, 118, 124
"Contract for Life", 65-6
Control, parental, 115
Controlled substance analogs
   (aka "designer drugs"), 38
Controlled substances, as
   designated by law, 37-8
Convenience stores, as locations
   for drug exchanges, 42
Coping strategies, teenagers'
   need to develop, 96
   with peer pressure and drugs, 138-9
   with stress, 18
Cost of various treatment options, 129
Counselling, treatment and
   aftercare, 119-34
Court costs, 141
Court system, juvenile, 141
Crack
   consequences of use, 74-5
   description of, 34-5
   excessive dangers of, 36
   influence on crime, 36
Crack usage, increases in, (8)
Crime, as effect of drug addiction, 36
Criminal charges, 140
   alcohol, 141-2
   cocaine, 142
   drunk driving, 61-2
   marijuana, 142
   obtaining/using false ID, 142
   possession of drug paraphernalia, 142
   possible, after keg parties, 55-6
Criminal liabilities
   drunk driving, 60-1
   keg parties, 55
Crisis/emergency, parental handling
   of, 122
Curfews, 90-1, 117, 141
Curriculum, schools, drug prevention, 100

D
Dealers, drug, (8)
Decision-making skills,
   helping teen develop, 73
Denial, 119-20
Dependency, 104
Depression, 146
Designated driver, 66
Designer drugs, facts about, 37-9
Diagnosis of drug abuse, 121
Discussion guidelines
   alcohol and drug use, 71-2
   experimentation, 108-12
   intervention, 122-4
   recreational use, 113-15
   social use of drugs/alcohol, 113-15
   teenage drinking, 67
   undesirable friends, 117
Diseases linked to alcohol abuse, 27
Drinking, social and recreational, 25
Drinking and driving
   (see also "drunk driving")
   statistics, 60
   teen responsibility, 64

(drinking and driving, continued)
   teenage, 58-66
Driving under influence of drugs, 59-60
Drug abuse treatments, types
   available, 125-9
Drug dealers, (8)
Drug education in schools, 22-3
Drug facts, parents' awareness of, 23
Drug paraphernalia, 23
   as evidence of drug use, 105
Drug prevention curriculum, 100
Drug testing, 113
   kits, 118
Drug tolerance, 102
Drug use
   frequency of, 102
   symptoms of, 104-5
Drug/alcohol combinations,
   effects of, 39, 59-60
Drugged driving, 59-60
Drugs,
   availability of, 38
   chemical patterns for, 38-9
   definition of, 19-20
Drunk driving
   as cause of death among
      adolescents, (8)
   conviction, loss of license, 64
   criminal charges, 61-2
   criminal liabilities, 60-1
   effect of beer/keg parties, 58
   insurance liabilities, 60-1
   parental liability, 62
DUI (driving under the influence)
   conviction, 158
   statutes, 59-60
DuPont, Jr., M.D., Robert L., 19, 79, 116

E
Ecstasy, a designer drug, 37
Education, teachers, symptoms
   of drug use, 100
Effective communication, need for, 80-1
Emergency back-up, by parents, 96
Emergency situations, coping with, 109
Emotional effects of marijuana, 30
Evaluations, free, 126
Excessive parental control, 95
Experimentation
   accepting the possibility of, 107-8
   discussion guidelines, 108-12
   suggested counter-actions, 107-8
   teenager-initiated discussion, 110
Experimenter, definition of, 102

F
False IDs, 23, 142
Family
   as refuge for the teenager, 77
   intervention, 122-3
   involvement, need for in treatment, 128
   responsibility in intervention, 100-01
   role in prevention of alcohol abuse, 70-1
Family activities, 94, 114
Fast food outlets, as locations
   for drug exchanges, 43
Financial responsibility, by teenager, 96

INDEX | 177

For Kids Only, 134-9
Free evaluations, 126
Frequency of drug use, 102
Friend's parent's problem with drugs, 147
Friend's problem with drugs, 136-7
Friends
  doing something illegal, 140
  of children, importance of knowing, 82
  undesirable, 83, 140

G
Gateway drugs, (7)
Getting Tough on Gateway Drugs, 79
Goals
  setting for social users, 114
  setting for teenagers, 78-9
Grapevine network, parents', 84
Guidelines
  parental, for keg party control, 56-7
  social, for teenagers, 89-90

H
Hallucinogenic drugs, 38
Hangin' out, 41
  alternatives to, 92
  precautions from police, 139-142
Hashish, 19
Health effects of alcohol abuse, 26-7
Health insurance, applicability of, 129
Health problems associated with marijuana, 31
Help, asking for, 120
Help for parents, 120-34
Home Aftercare Contract, 131
Homeowners insurance, settling post-keg party claims, 55
Homeowners policy, liability limits, 159
Homes without parental supervision, 45-6
Host liability, beer/keg parties, 55-6
Hosting alcohol/drug-free teenage party, 151-2
Hotel/motel parties, unchaperoned, 47
Households, substance abusing, incidence of, (8)
How to Give a Successful Teenage Party, 151-2

I
ID, false, 23, 142
Idealism in adolescents, 16-7
Illegal possession, as criminal charge, 43
Informed parent, best weapon against abuse, 71
Inhalants, 19
Inpatient treatment programs, 126-9
Inpatient vs. outpatient treatment, 127
Insurance considerations, 158-160
Insurance liabilities, drunk driving, 60-1
Intervention, 99-118
  family's responsibility, 100-01
  family, 122-3
  parents' responsibility, 103
  school involvement in, 99-100, 119
  with advanced user, 115-18
  with drug abuser, 122
  with recreational user, 112-15
Intervention specialist, 123

J
Journal of the American Medical Association, 20
Juvenile court system, 141
Juvenile law system, 154

K
Keg parties, 48-58
  (see also "beer parties")
  absentee parents, 48
  availability of drugs, 48, 52
  description of, 48-9
  destructive aspects, 52
  effect on drunk driving, 58
  effects of, 51
  legal liabilities, 55-6
  police "bust" of, 53
  possible criminal charges, 55-6
  prevention and control, 46, 56-7
  profit potential, 51
  scenario, 49-50
  supervision by parents, attitude of, 51-2
  why teenagers go, 53-4
Keg party control, parental guidelines, 56-7
Kits, drug testing, 118

L
Legal expenses, 141
Legal liabilities, 140-1
  of alcohol use, 70
  parents, for teenager actions, 124
Legal precautions, 139-142
Legal procedures, 141
  for minors, 153
Letting go, knowing when & how, 95-8
Liabilities, legal, keg parties, 55-6
Liability, parental, 154
Liability limits, homeowner's policy, 159
Loss of interest, as symptom of drug use, 105
Loss of license, as effect of drunk driving, 61, 64
Love, unconditional, importance of, 96
LSD and other hallucinogenic drugs, 19, 38

M
Macdonald, Donald Ian, M.D., 34, 125
MADD (Mothers Against Drunk Driving), 86
Malls, shopping, as drug "market", 41-2
Mann, Peggy, 31
Marijuana, 19
  average age of first use, (8)
  "burnout", 30-1
  effects when combined with alcohol, 31
  facts about, 29-31
Marijuana Alert, 31
Modern drugs, potency of, 23, 37
Money and drug/alcohol use, 91
Money management, by teens, 91-2

N
Narcotics, 19
Narcotics Anonymous, 132

178 | INDEX

National Federation of Parents
  for Drug-free Youth, 86
National Institute on Drug Abuse, 116
Negative role models, 78
Neighborhood efforts at prevention, 82-4
Neighborhood network of parents, 84-5
Networking parents, 85-6
Newton, Miller, Ph.D., 125
Nicotine, facts about, 27-9

O

Open door policy, importance of, 82
Out of control situation,
  definition of, 122

P

Paraphernalia, drug, 23
  as evidence of drug use, 105
Parent, informed, 71
Parent support groups, aftercare, 131
Parent-approved beer parties, 46
Parent-supervised keg party, 51-2
Parent/police cooperation, 57-8
Parental attitudes, keg parties, 51-2
Parental authority, 74
Parental availability, 74, 80
Parental awareness,
  alcohol/drug use, 71-81
Parental consistency,
  importance of, 72
Parental control, 95, 115
Parental counter-actions, 107-8
Parental denial, 119-20
Parental handling of
  crisis/emergency, 122
Parental legal liability for
  teenager actions, 124
Parental liability, 56, 154
  for teenager drunk driving, 62
Parental peer pressure, 72, 84
Parental supervision
  absence of, 45-6
  of teen parties, 91
Parental use of alcohol/drugs,
  78, 106, 109
Parenting, preventive, 107
Parents
  awareness of drug facts, 23
  Awareness Test, 146-7
  grapevine network, 84
  influence on peer groups, 104
  involvement with teens in
    community projects, 86
  motives in exerting authority, 72
  networking, 84-6
  responsibilities, teen drinking
    and driving, 63-4
  responsibility, 103
  single, notes for, 87-9
Parents of teen's friends,
  importance of knowing, 83
Parks and ball fields, as locations
  for drug exchanges, 44-5
Peer groups, 17-8
  adolescents, 14
  parents' influence on, 104
Peer pressure, 102, 106, 111, 116, 141
  among teenagers, 73

(peer pressure, continued)
  in grade school, (8)
  parental, 72, 84
  positive, 136-7, 138
Peer relationships, 41
Peer support groups, aftercare, 131
Personality/mood changes,
  adolescent, 15-6, 146
Phencyclidine (PCP), 19
Physical appearance changes, as
  symptoms of drug use, 105
Physical changes in adolescents, 15
Physical signs of abuse, 146
Police action on beer/keg parties,
  53, 140
Police record, 141
Police/parent cooperation, 57-8
Porter, Dr. Bill, 120
Positive relationships,
  importance of, 77
Positive role models, 78
Pot parties, after school, 45-6
Potency of modern drugs, 23, 37
Potential Legal Liabilities of
  the "Kegger" Scenario, 154-7
Praise, importance of, 72-3, 75-6
Prescription drugs/alcohol
  effect on driving, 39
Prevention and control of keg
  parties, 56-7
Prevention efforts in the
  community, 85-6
Preventive parenting, 107
PRIDE, 86
Problem, advanced use, definition
  of, 118
Problem situations for teens,
  checklist, 134-6
Problem teenage drinkers,
  incidence of, (8)
Procuring drugs for minor,
  criminal charge, 43

R

Rationalizations, teenager, 120
Reasons for drug and alcohol use, 20-1
Recreational use of drugs,
  parental enforcement against, 113
  parental penalties for, 113
Recreational user, 103
  dealing with, 112-15
REDDI (Report Every Drunk
  Driver Immediately), 65
Refusal of treatment by teenager, 124
Relationships, positive, importance of, 77
Religion, role in drug use prevention, 79
Reproductive system, effect of
  marijuana on, 31
Resolving conflicts, 81
Respect for teenagers' feelings, 81
Responsibilities, teenagers, as
  citizens, 140-1
Responsibility, developing in
  teenagers, 73-4
Rewards, for behavior, 72-3, 114
Right to make choices, teenagers, 95
Risks of early use, alcohol, 67

INDEX

Role models, importance of, 77-8
Rules, home/school, disregard of, 149

S

SADD (Students Against Drunk Driving), 65, 86
School issues and activities, 85-6
School performance, decline in, 146
School programs, intervention teams, 100
School support groups, aftercare, 133
School's involvement
 in aftercare, 132-3
 in drug education, 22-3
 in treatment, 120-1
 in intervention, 99-100
School-sponsored alternative activities, 94
Search, when appropriate, 101
Second opinion, 121, 127
Seeking assistance, 125-6
Self-confidence, helping teenager build, 75-6
Self-esteem, 75-6, 80
Self-help groups, 127, 132, 138
Serving others, importance of to teenagers, 98
Sex, teenage, influence of drug/alcohol use, 21
Sexual development, effects of marijuana on, 30
Shoplifting, 140
Shopping Malls as drug "market", 41-2
Signs/symptoms of addiction, 103
Single parents, notes for, 87-9
Sleeping over, aka "slumber parties", 46-7
Smokeless tobacco, 28-9
Snuff, 29
Social alcohol/drug use, 112-13
Social drinking, 25
Social guidelines for teenagers, 89-90
Social interaction, teenagers' need for, 42, 54
Social needs, teenagers, 78
Social norms, among teenagers, 41
Social relationships, 83
Specific Signs and Symptoms of Adolescent Drug Use, 148-9
Stages of Drug Abuse, 150
Statistics, drinking and driving, 60
Step-parents, notes for, 88
Stress management as learned skill, 22-3
Stress, adolescent, 18, 22
Substance Abuse Policy and Procedure, School, 162-170
Substance abusing households, incidence of, (8)
Suicide, teenage, influence of drug/alcohol use, 21-2
Supervision of teen parties by parents, 91
Support group, aftercare, 100
Symptoms of abuse, 148-9
Symptoms of drug use, 104-5

T

Teacher education, symptoms of drug use, 100
Teen Clubs, as alternatives to "hangin' out", 43-4
Teen efforts to combat drinking and driving, 65-6
Teen money management, 91-2
Teen responsibility, drinking and driving, 64
Teenage denial, 120
Teenage drinking and driving, 58-66
 parents' responsibilities, 63-4
Teenage drinking
 discussion guidelines, 67
 the case against, 67-70
Teenage problem drinkers, incidence of, (8)
Teenage refusal of treatment 123
Teenage sex, influence of drug/alcohol use, 21
Teenage suicide, influence of drug/alcohol use, 21-2
Teenager's financial responsibility, 96
Teenagers most susceptible to drug use and abuse, 20
Teenagers
 feelings, respect for, 81
 perceptions of parents and other adults, 47
 right to make choices, 95
 serving others, 86
 social needs, 78
Testing for drugs, 113
THC (marijuana's psychoactive ingredient), 19, 30
The Clinical Syndrome of Adolescent Drug Abuse, 125
Tobacco, smokeless, 28-9
Tolerance, of drugs, 102
Tranquilizers, 19
Treatment
 aftercare, 130-4
 inpatient vs. outpatient, 127
 types available, 125-9
Treatment center, 123
Treatment groups, self-help, 127
Treatment options, cost of, 129
Treatment programs, inpatient, 126
Trust, 72, 83

U

Unconditional love, importance of, 96
Undesirable friends, 83, 140
Urine screening, 118
User
 adolescent, compared to other adolescents, 106-7
 advanced, 115-18
 definition of, 103

V

Value system, helping teenager establish, 79
Vandalism, 140
Vehicular assault, as result of drunk driving, 61-2
Vehicular homicide, as result of drunk driving, 61-2

W

Withdrawal symptoms, 148

ABOUT THE AUTHORS

Anne Swany Harrity

A graduate of Duke University, Anne Harrity has been a resident of Aurora, Colorado since 1972 when she resigned from IBM (after ten years as a systems engineer) to become a full-time wife and mother.

Since then she has been very active in community affairs, particularly those relating to teenage alcohol and drug problems. Currently she holds a volunteer position as Director of Development for the Addiction Research and Treatment Services Foundation University of Colorado).

Anne is married and has two children and two step-children.

Ann Brey Christensen

Ann Christensen grew up in Denver, Colorado, attended Connecticut College for Women, and graduated from the University of Denver.

After graduation she was employed by IBM as a systems analyst. She resigned to raise a family and became extensively involved in community volunteer work — particularly in the local schools.

As a board member of the Overland Community Task Force on Youth and Drugs she joined with Anne Harrity to research and write the booklet that led to kids, Drugs, & Alcohol. Ann works today as a teacher and counselor.